SENIOR HIGH VOL. 6
Pacesetter

The Complete Youth Ministry Resource

Friends

BECOMING A FRIEND FINDER AND KEEPER

∎

David C. Cook Publishing Co.

Elgin, Illinois/Weston, Ontario

Senior High
PACESETTER

◼

FRIENDS
Becoming a Friend
Finder and Keeper

DAVID C. COOK PUBLISHING CO.
Elgin, Illinois/Weston, Ontario
FRIENDS—Becoming a Friend
Finder and Keeper

◼

Creative Team

Project Editor: Kevin A. Miller
Editors: Anne E. Dinnan; Paul N.
Woods
Assistant Editor: Eric Potter
Designer: Jill Ellen Novak

◼

Management Team

David C. Cook III, Editor in Chief
Joseph Bayly, President
Ralph Gates, Director of Church
Resources
Marlene D. LeFever, Executive Edi-
tor of Ministry Resources
Jim Townsend, Bible Editor
Gregory Eaton Clark, Director of
Design Services

◼

Scripture quotations, unless other-
wise noted, are from the *Holy Bi-
ble: New International Version.* ©
1978 New York International Bible
Society. Used by permission of
Zondervan Bible Publishers.
*We'd like to thank the many
encouragers who helped PACE-
SETTER become reality. —The
Editors*
Published by David C. Cook Pub-
lishing Co.
850 North Grove Avenue
Elgin, Illinois 60120
Cable address: DCCOOK
First printing, 1986
Printed in the United States of
America
Library of Congress Catalog Card
Number: 85-72934
ISBN: 0-89191-329-7

Cover photo by Bakstad Photographics

Friends

BECOMING A FRIEND FINDER AND KEEPER

He was only a sophomore. His so-called friends were basically drinking buddies. He felt bored and left out. So it was no surprise that one night, while vandalizing a store with his friends, he drank a whole bottle of booze—fast.

The surprise was that when he regained consciousness he asked for Mike. He didn't want to telephone his dad or his friends. He wanted to talk to a young man he had met only a month before, a "really neat guy named Mike."

When Mike got the call, he left work and headed for the hospital to see this teenager whose life he had unknowingly so impacted. Mike remembered the awkwardness of walking up to the sophomore and introducing himself. He recalled the strained silences as he tried to find out more about him. And how, after the initial suspicion was overcome, that high school kid had begun to open up over a Coke or in the front yard when he swung by to say hi.

They hadn't really talked about "spiritual things," but there was no hesitation from this sophomore when Mike asked if he could pray for healing and help. Mike had become a significant, caring adult to that lonely, lost teenager.

We can never know the full impact we might have if we are willing to befriend teenagers. Friendship from both peers and adults is critical to young people. Making and keeping friends is their most basic survival skill.

As caring adults, we can help kids learn the essentials of committed friendship—especially as they see that type of friendship in us.

INSIDE ▪ THIS ▪ VOLUME

FRIENDS: Becoming a Friend Finder and Keeper (Volume Six in the PACESETTER series) can help you lead your group into solid, long-lasting friendships.

First, for background on the topic and your own enrichment, we offer "Expert Insights," articles by leaders in youth ministry. For example, how do you teach kids basic friendship skills? Check out the article by peer-counseling authority Dr. Barbara Varenhorst. What's behind dating? Get the inside look from sociologist Dr. Anthony Campolo. Youth worker Jim Burns offers insights from his experience on how to help the friendless kid in your group.

Then, use PACESETTER's practical programming tools:

▪ The "Meetings" section gives you five complete meeting plans on friendship-related topics. Reproduce the activity pieces at the back of this book for use with these.

▪ Then there's the "More Bright Ideas" section. Here you'll find around 20 activity ideas, many suitable as meetings in themselves.

▪ Need material for an upcoming retreat? You'll find it in "Breakaway": a powerful retreat to help kids think through guy-girl relationships.

▪ Need a meaningful drama for a youth night or service that's almost here? Turn to the "Kids in the Spotlight" section for an insightful piece called "Class Clones."

▪ Finally, to help you keep good friendships within your group, we've included "Nurturing Your Group" by Dr. Gary Downing.

So if you're looking at a blank calendar and wondering what you're going to do with your kids, you've come to the right place. Whether you need one activity or months of programs, PACESETTER is at your service. □

Contents

Contents

Illustration by Paul Yalowitz

Solving the Friendship Mystery

Teaching your kids basic friendship skills

THERE'S A STORY ABOUT A LITTLE

girl who didn't want to be left alone at bedtime.

"You've got your doll," said her mother. "Your doll will keep you company."

"When I'm lonely," the child replied, "a doll is no good. I want someone with skin on."

Having someone with skin on is a universal need. And, for young people, it is their emotional life blood—not just when lonely, but also when they have a problem, need to talk, or want the security of a companion at school events, parties, or just walking down the hall. Most of all youth need *someone* to give them the identity of being a friend of someone.

But many, *many* people—not just youths, don't really know how to make friends.

BY BARBARA B. VARENHORST

Expert Insights

Though we encounter models of friendship almost daily, mystery and confusion still exist about how to make and keep friends. Age does not seem to increase ability. Rather, the art of friendship making requires mentors, practice, growth in self-appreciation, and often some painful experiences.

Teaching youth how to understand the mystery and deal with the confusion of making friends, therefore, is a major aspect of Christian ministry to them. Their lives center around this need, and so does their understanding of a relationship with Christ. It is very difficult for young people to understand God's love for them, or to believe that they have a friend in Jesus, if they have never had a real human friend.

The task of teaching friendship skills, however, is difficult simply because of the nature of adolescence. Friends must feel that they have something to contribute, or that there are

> ### *Friendships can't be demanded, manipulated, or bought.*

reasons why they might be appreciated as friends. Many adolescents lack these feelings of self-worth, and this prevents them from initiating a friendship. Often it causes them to do or say things that destroy friendship. However, because of their great desire, and great need, young people eagerly respond to any help they can get in learning how to be a more effective friend.

In teaching these basic skills to young people, I always use an informal setting that includes group discussions, learning activities, some lecture, and ''homework'' to push students to practice what I am teaching. I also deal with basic motivations and attitudes, both in what I say, and indirectly through how I teach specific skills.

Motivation and Attitudes

A course on friendship making should begin with a discussion of why young people want to make friends. Friendships, for kids, are often a means to an end—of feeling more important, being more secure, having someone to turn to, or having companionship. There is nothing wrong with these *desires*, except that they are the wrong motives to start friendships with. Kids have to learn that friends are to be loved and things are to be used. Friendships can't be demanded, manipulated, or bought.

This means that your students have to begin to shift their thoughts from themselves to how they can give friendship to others, especially those who need a friend the most. When they start approaching relationships with the motivation of *giving*, rather than receiving, much of their self-consciousness disappears, and their approach to others becomes sincere.

I do a group activity where I ask students to think about current or past friends they have had whom they value. If they haven't had such a friend, I ask them to think about the kind of friend they would like to have. Then I ask them to share with the group as a whole the qualities or attributes of that friend. In this sharing, it becomes evident that the giving of friendship *first* has always been a key element. If negative actions or

qualities are mentioned, these, too, can be used to emphasize the importance of negating self-interest in exchange for a genuine interest in another. It is also meaningful to relate such a discussion to how Christ gives friendship to us.

Attitudes About Self

Sometimes I videotape students to show how their expressions affect others. I often wonder if they realize how much their bodies express a lack of desire to be a friend. When a boy smiles with his mouth *and* his eyes, you don't see the braces he is wearing. A straight posture and brisk walk blots out acne that may be blossoming on a face. Yet so many young people don't use this simple way of attracting friends, because they often are inwardly concentrating on all the things that are wrong with them.

It's hard to smile, I agree, when your mouth is full of metal, or your face is blotched with pimples. Yet when kids tell me about friends they really like, I find those things seldom matter. So we talk about what makes friends attracted to one another. I ask them to practice different facial expressions alone, in front of their mirrors. Then I ask them to try smiling at five different strangers during the next week and record what effect this had on *them,* as well as on the person at whom they smiled.

This attitude towards self also leads to the way we can affirm or compliment others. Since we value receiving compliments from those we respect, it follows that, in developing friendships, it's important to learn how to give affirmation to others.

Taking one person at a time, each person in the group expresses something they like or appreciate about the focus person, even if it is only the color of the dress or shirt she or he is wearing. They have all been prepared to do this in a very serious and sincere way.

The results are fantastic! Young people emerge from the group walking taller because they have *heard* positive things from their peers! It is a high that carries them through many weeks, and even months. Based on their reaction, they are asked to attempt to give three sincere compliments to others throughout the week.

Skills

How to Start a Conversation

The most basic skill in friendship making is how to start a conversation. It is amazing to me how long kids can sit next to one another on a school bus, at a party, or even in youth groups and never talk to someone they haven't known before. Even many of those who attend youth groups regularly may not know the names of those who also are regular members. This reluctance is often because they don't know *how* to start conversations. Unfortunately, they miss many potential friends.

When asked why they don't initiate conversations with people they don't know, I get various reasons: They are afraid they won't know what to say; they think the other person might not want to talk to them; the person they approach might think they are weird or probing into their privacy. Most of these reasons come from the negative feelings they have about themselves, or their concern about what others will think of *them*. I use these reasons to point out that not being friendly, not reaching out to others, is a basic type of self-centeredness.

I ask students to pair off and hold a conversation for ten minutes. Their reactions to doing this are discussed in the total group. Then I review guidelines based on what they did or didn't do as they practiced starting conversations with partners.

1. *Introduce yourself first, stating your name clearly and proudly!* Sometimes young people act as though they've forgotten their names, or they want them to be a well-kept secret. Sharing your name is a beginning gesture of friendliness.

2. *Open the conversation with a topic of mutual interest.* An opening topic may be an item of clothing another is wearing; a record both are listening to; or even why they are where they are (waiting for a bus, sitting at a party, etc.).

3. *Ask for information.* Asking questions can demonstrate interest, as well as give free information that can be used to develop the conversation. In asking how long the person has lived in the area, free information might be where he lived before, why she came to the area, or a family's occupation. Picking up on one of these topics not only shows you are listening, but it helps to develop the sharing between you. However, if you ask questions of another, it is also important to volunteer similar information about yourself to avoid the feeling of being interviewed.

4. *Ask open questions.* Everyone seems to know how to ask the "Have you? Do you? Are you?" closed questions that often get one word or one sentence answers. If you want to get to know someone at a more personal level and allow another to share with you, then you need to know how and when to ask open questions. These are questions that ask "What makes . . .? When

have you . . .? Where do you . . .? How does it . . .?" about a personal interest, experience, or activity. These questions create opportunities to share meaningful information that is important for developing friendships.

In pairs, have students practice asking open questions by interviewing one another about a personal interest or hobby. Then they can practice doing this with family members at home during

> *Not being friendly is a basic type of self-centeredness.*

the next week and share their experiences at the next meeting. My students often are excited about the results, and even parents report a change in the kinds of conversations they are beginning to have as a family.

How to Listen with Acceptance

Listening with acceptance means letting another talk without interruption or impatience, even when the other rambles or repeats himself in an effort to express what he is feeling. It involves not interjecting personal comments or telling a *better* story that changes the subject or focus of attention. It also involves not cutting off what the other is saying by offering quick advice, such as, "You shouldn't feel that way." Learning to do this requires a willingness to put aside one's own desire for attention, as well as a training of self to focus totally on the other person.

Another aspect of listening, however, involves learning how to explore the meaning of what another is saying. This involves asking the other to explain her use of certain words, often ones we use frequently and vaguely. One time in a group discussion an eighth-grade boy referred to a teacher as a "nerd." Before judging him for using this label, I asked him to explain what he meant by that term. He explained that the teacher was unfair and inconsistent in the way she treated students. My questioning led to his telling me of feelings that would not have been revealed if I had only criticized his name-calling.

Ask students to take turns talking about something that concerns them. Then ask others in the group to say what they understood the person to have said and why. Often they are shocked at the misunderstanding that results from a misinterpretation of words. If this is done frequently, young people begin to acquire the habit of exploring more deeply what is said to them.

How to Care Without Hurting

If a friend has unintentionally hurt you, or has a habit or trait that really bugs you, what do you do? Usually the guilty person is the last one to hear about it, or learns about it when you explode in anger and say things you later regret.

When young people talk about broken friendships, often the cause was an inability to discuss a troublesome issue. They don't want to hurt their friend, or they're afraid their friend might get mad at them. But that is exactly what happens because they *don't* talk it out. Actually real friendship is demonstrated by risking another's anger in order to share feelings about what the other is doing.

It is such an important friendship skill that I teach a four-step process which requires much preparation and practice before it is

used. The process involves: 1) Describing an incident that illustrates the issue, one that has happened to you, not to someone else. 2) Explaining how you felt when this happened. The statement of *feelings* is important. 3) Specifying how you would like to be treated, or what changes you want. Often we criticize another and assume our friend knows what to do differently. Sometimes he or she doesn't, and a clear explanation of what you want can be helpful. 4) Explaining what you will do or feel that is positive if the friend does change, as well as what will happen if there is no change. There are always negative consequences if annoying issues are not resolved, and these consequences need to be expressed.

This process requires practice—and courage. When it is used, however, friendships can be saved. Also, it opens the path to forgiveness. Somehow until young people can learn to confront in love and then forgive, they can't really understand or accept God's love and forgiveness of us.

The Tests of Friendship

— ■ —

Perhaps the thing that is hardest for young people to understand is that before a friendship is for real, it has to be tested.

Ask young people to talk about what happens to a close friendship when a third person becomes involved. They all know what you mean because they have all experienced it. Usually the least secure in the friendship is the one who may compete by putting down the newcomer, gossiping about him or her, or becoming very possessive and demanding. Sometimes this works to maintain the relationship, but the real quality of friendship is missing. We never

win in friendships by hurting others or demanding loyalty.

The triangle situation is the most common way in which real friendship is tested. By being friendly and offering acceptance to a new friend, one learns how significant the original friendship really is. If it can be maintained while including others, then you've gained a real trust that is lasting. If the friendship becomes less close, or even ceases, you can move on to other friendships. Of course there is hurt involved, but perhaps not as deep or lasting as there might have been if negative ways were used to hold on.

Another test of friendship is being loyal to a friend by speaking up to defend him or her, or by not listening to gossip or unkind things. Helping young people learn what to say when feeling pressure from a group is a useful exercise. Hearing themselves actually say the words in the presence of others may lead them to do it when faced with that pressure.

The costs of friendship are hard for young people to think about. Through discussions, Bible study, and practice, however, students can be challenged to face those costs for the sake of acquiring the real friends they want, and becoming the friends they want to be. Push them to the challenge.

For me there is no more rewarding work than teaching friendship skills to youth. As I have done it, I have seen them grow to enjoy life more fully and deepen their spiritual lives. I've also made many friends among the youth I've taught. Your efforts in doing this *will* be a true ministry to them. □

Barbara B. Varenhorst, Ph.D., *author of the book,* Real Friends, *is director of the Palo Alto Peer Counseling Center in Palo Alto, California.*

A Kid's-Eye View on Peer Pressure

One can find peer pressure in so many different situations other than the obvious clichéd ones like taking a drink at a party because everyone else is, and you don't want to be the only one not.

I look at peer pressure as being forced out of individualism into conforming to a *group* decision. It's really hard to avoid because nobody wants to feel left out of anything. But it feels great when I can say, "No, I'd rather . . ." It isn't always bad to me to stay home and be by myself instead of going out with friends, but I am always free to make whatever decision I want.

A big peer pressure I have in my life is not wanting to let my friends down, or feeling like I am not doing my share in the activities I am involved in. For instance, driving is always a hassle. If no one can drive, I usually volunteer without checking first. And that can stir up waves at home. Or, at committee meetings, I am always volunteering to do things that no one else is willing to do, 'til I get totally bogged down. It is very difficult for me to say, "No, I'm sorry, but I just can't."

There are positive and negative ways to look at peer pressure. The positive would be peer pressure that helps people—like deciding to do something as a group to benefit the group or someone else. For instance, in a pep band a few people plan to dress up and do different things to promote spirit and make the pep band more fun. No one wants to feel left out, so usually everyone dresses up. On the positive side, this does promote spirit. But it could also be negative because the group is not allowing an individual to not dress up without feeling like an outcast.

I think it's always a struggle to find a median between the positive and negative sides of peer pressure.

Andrea Schmitz is a high school senior in Elgin, Illinois. She is active in her church and serves on her denomination's commission on youth for her area. Andrea works in the gift shop of a hospital and plans to attend college in the fall.

Pair Bonding

Bonding is the "glue" by which God unites men and women in marriage. Psychologists have identified a 12-step process for ideal bonding. Too often we (kids especially) rush past these six vital steps, and pain— sometimes tragedy—is the result.

1. *Eye to body.* This is not a "sexual look." It is the "Eureka!" look of discovery.
2. *Eye to eye.* In the discovery of a potential relationship, the eye contact is brief.
3. *Voice to voice.* Today's family often installs a second private line to accommodate to the importance of voice to voice.
4. *Hand to hand.* The couple makes a social statement. "The two of us are together."
5. *Arm to shoulder.* There is a gesture of "ownership" in the arm around the shoulder. It extends the social statement: "We have a special relationship."
6. *Arm to waist.* The couple at this point pull their bodies close.

During this sixth step, a decision about the future of the relationship is urgent. This is the "last exit" on the pair-bonding freeway. Any "emergency exits" down the road will almost certainly leave skid marks of grief and pain.

From a review by Kris Tomasik *of* Bonding: Relationships in the Image of God *(Word, 1985) in* CAMPUS LIFE Leader's Guide.

Must Men Be Friendless?

When asked, "How many men have real friends?" the leading psychologists and therapists in this country answer about ten percent. Most males view other men as allies at best and enemies at worst. Men are expected to compete, whether the setting is the tennis court or the law court. That almost ensures the relationship will stay at a superficial, guarded level. Like the turtle, only when a sense of safety prevails, will men slowly relax into a genuine friendship. *By Paul D. Robbins. From* Leadership, *Fall 1984.*

The Dating Games

Why girls and guys relate the way they do

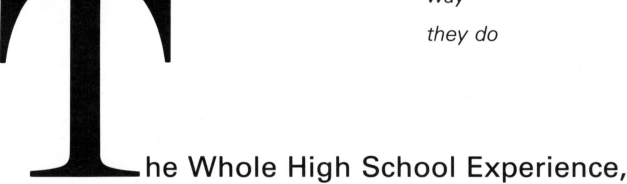

T he Whole High School Experience,

particularly the senior year, can be understood only in terms of guys trying to pressure girls, and girls trying to pressure guys. So argues Martin Friedenberg in *Coming of Age in America.* And he's right. Who has the prestige in high school? The good students? The athletes? Not necessarily. The kids who are popular with the opposite sex have the prestige.

Being on the basketball team only helps your prestige insofar as being on the basketball team enhances your image with the opposite sex. That is one reason why guys participate on basketball and football teams. If you wanted to play the game the last thing you would *ever* do is go out for the team. Because you don't get to play! You get to practice and practice and run drills and run drills. But only five guys get to play. Most guys that go out for the team sit on the bench. Why do they do it? Because there's something about being on the varsity team. It adds status, but more than that, it attracts girls.

Here's Friedenberg's interesting observation: One's status with *the guys* is determined by how one is doing with *the girls!* The other guys will not necessarily think a guy is terrific if he's on the basketball team. But if he's a "10" in the eyes of the girls, not only do the girls like him, but the other guys like him. The way guys view another guy is always in terms of how they think the *girls* perceive him.

This phenomenon is even more true for girls: the other girls will often see a particular girl in terms of how they think the guys perceive her.

B Y T O N Y C A M P O L O

with Paul Woods

The Games Kids Play

The whole social system in the high school is caught up with sex games. The primary way to earn social acceptance is by being popular with the opposite sex. When you achieve popularity with members of the opposite sex, you enhance your status with members of your own sex. And the implications of that are very tough to deal with. Guys often won't date girls whom they find interesting, bright, and witty. Why? Because those girls don't have high status with most of the guys in the school. Consequently, guys won't date somebody they *do* like, and often will date somebody they *don't* like—simply because of what their peers will think. A girl ends up being dated not because she is liked, but because of what dating her means within the social system of the school. There are a lot of hurt feelings and a lot of emotional hardships that go with that. The dating game is, primarily, people *using* other people to enhance their status within the system.

Lionel Tiger, one of the great anthropologists of our time, recognized a related problem in the socialization of teenagers: guys are trained to be committed to a group, while girls are trained to be committed to an individual. A girl generally has a best girl friend and a guy has the gang. It's probably related to the games that we teach kids to play. Girls play solitary games. They get their best girl friends and go to their rooms and play with their dolls. But boys are taught team games. Everything takes place in a group context for guys; for girls everything takes place in solitude or with their best friends. This social training creates a number of problems in high school.

> # The dating game is, primarily, people using other people.

Friends and Foes

One problem is that this system can make girls into horrendous gossips. A girl has a best girl friend. All of a sudden this girl friend starts talking with and being friends with another girl. With guys it's no serious problem. But this is the destruction of the girl's whole social world. This is her *life*! You say, "Well, don't be so selfish." But as the girl sees it, her whole life is in jeopardy. And her defense is to start running down the other girl. This is where the gossip begins. And it can get nasty! It is the girl's *one* defense mechanism to preserve her social world.

Guys, on the other hand, are often incredibly loyal. Here's the difference: Suppose there were eight guys hanging around together and one was dating a particular girl. If one of his buddies saw that he really didn't like her very much, would the buddy go ahead and date her? He *might* under one condition: that he would ask the guy first. "Hey, I noticed things are cooling off with you and Sue. How would you feel if I dated her?"

Guys would generally ask permission. But few girls would

ever ask permission of another girl about getting a date. They can cut each other's throats. It's fortunate for guys—they've got a very, very positive, affirming socialization process.

The Seduction Game

However, this socialization process also causes problems when it comes to dating. When a guy begins to leave his group and gets.interested in a girl, the group puts tremendous pressure on him to come back to the group. So the girl has got a real problem. She not only has to worry about how she is going over with the guy, but also about how she can get the guy away from his group. Interestingly enough, there is a primary reason a guy can leave the group and go after a girl that will earn him status in the eyes of the guys, and that is if she is putting out for him sexually. The guy often feels he must communicate to his peers that he is getting all kinds of sexual favors—whether he actually is or not. It's the only way he can justify leaving the group.

That message is not lost on the girl. Therefore, the girl is walking a tightrope: How can she be seductive enough to get the guy away from his group and to justify his leaving the group, without getting seduced? It's easy for a minister to say, "Don't get involved sexually. When you go on a date, don't do this; don't do that; don't do the other thing." But the whole social structure in high school is one in which the girl's primary role is to be seductive enough to get a guy without getting seduced. That is a pretty hard job for a 17-year old.

Let's illustrate this problem. A guy and a girl are out on a date. Suddenly the guy begins to move, and the girl says, "Hey! What makes you think I'm interested in *this*?" And the guy is furious!

"What do you mean?" he says. "You've been sending out signals for three weeks. You've been coming on like gang busters! And suddenly when I get you in the back of the car, you say no?" She had no intention of getting into that situation. But she had to be seductive to win the guy.

I don't know that the church has ever spoken to this problem. We've told people not to get into compromising situations, but we've never dealt with the real problem. And there aren't any easy answers.

Power or Love?

We're dealing with a *power* problem here, too. All of us by nature want to be in positions of power. In the dating relationship, whoever is least interested has the most power. The one who really loves loses power. So it is never safe for the guy to like the girl more than the girl likes him. And vice versa. Because that makes one very vulnerable. Thus we have to play this game of pretending we're not interested when we desperately are. Think of the pain! All of us are afraid to lose power. None of us want to become vulnerable. So the game goes on. In the end, teenagers are much more willing to trust in power than they are to trust in love.

In a real sense, the message of the Gospel is the cessation of power games. Total surrender to love. Not only for God, but also love for one another. In a sense, the Gospel is the *end* of the dishonesty games. A good verse of Scripture for teenagers is James 5:12 (KJV): "Let your yea be yea; and your nay, nay." Honesty in relationships can help to end the cruel games kids play.

Breaking Up

Another problem with the dating game is that most dating relationships come to an end. Between the ages of 13 and 19 the average teenager falls in love six times. These are not little emotional binges, but heart-aching, mind-boggling, totally consuming love relationships. And most end with one person being dumped. There will be few things in the person's life that will bring as much agony and as much pain as the breaking of a teenage romance. And the absence of honesty in dating is revealed in breaking off. The girl, realizing that things are not working out, but not being able to articulate that, ends up trying to get rid of the guy by being mean. And he's hurt. Her yea is never yea and her nay is never nay. She claims there's nothing wrong. He can't figure what's going on. There's coldness, cruelty, and humiliation. She keeps on until the guy is forced to end the relationship. And then she blames him. Guys do the same thing to girls.

> The church ends up rejecting those who are the most rejected.

We ought to spend a lot of time helping kids learn *how* to break up, and how to handle it with grace, and dignity, and righteousness. Help kids develop a way of breaking up in which the two can still be friends when the romance is over.

Who's at Fault?

The American dating system is largely perpetuated by adults. We create the social system that necessitates kids having partners of the opposite sex. The minute an established school system sets up a senior prom and makes it the highlight of one's senior year, it has said, "If you're not dating, you're nothing." And it's a very serious problem. Some churches respond by having a dinner the night of the senior prom. But the offensiveness is still there. The big problem is not the dance, but forcing kids to be in a partnership with a member of the opposite sex. And when you set up a banquet the night of the senior prom, you are still saying that those who can't get dates can't come. The church ends up rejecting those who are the most rejected and glorifying those who are the most glorified. It's in complete contradiction to the Gospel.

A Viable Instrument

The Church is perhaps the only existing institution that can be a viable instrument for overcoming the dating system with all of its problems. I have seen many instances where a youth leader has been able to mold the youth group into such a cohesive unit that the group would rather go out together on a Saturday night than to go out on dates. When the youth group reaches that point, it makes little difference whether or not the Sunday evening program sticks.

Two high school students alone on a date are not conversationally adept enough to keep the evening interesting. So after about three hours they run out of things to say. That's when it becomes sexually dangerous. But it's great if the couple dates in the context of the group, because the group carries the evening. They will be much more relaxed and much more themselves. And they will get to know one another. Whether or not a person is beautiful is altered by what you get to know about the person. In group dating, some girls who are quite average begin to look quite beautiful; some beautiful girls begin to look quite average; and some guys who don't look like much become very handsome. In short, group dating allows kids to evaluate each other in areas that really matter. If a leader can build that cohesiveness, that sense of

> ## In group dating, some girls who are quite average begin to look quite beautiful.

caring, that feeling among kids that they have more fun together than they would have on a date, he or she has done something terrific! That is probably the most healthy contribution a youth worker can make to the socialization of his or her kids.

Our Challenge

I've looked at a lot of problems and only given a few answers. Maybe I've been a little like Moses—leading you around in the wilderness, but never bringing you to the Promised Land. The important thing is that all of us understand the issues involved, and with God's help do our best to work with kids in the light of that understanding. No one can rightfully ask more of us than that. □

Dr. Anthony Campolo *is the chairman of the Department of Sociology at Eastern College in St. Davids, Pennsylvania. He is a popular speaker, author of numerous books, and is featured in several videos, including* Present Shock *(Cook).*

Paul Woods *is editor of Youth Publications at David C. Cook Publishing Co.*

Technical Virginity

When researchers began to study sexuality in the evangelical community, they came up with a special category: the "technical virgin."

This is the young Christian who knows that you're to save intercourse for marriage, so he or she does everything else but. Petting, touching, even getting undressed and making love in the nude, without ever going all the way. The question: Is he or she a virgin? What the researchers found was that there is a significant sector of

the female evangelical community that was more sexually experienced than large groups of people who had had sexual intercourse. These people were sexually sophisticated, but had never had intercourse because the Bible called that fornication.

When it comes to sexuality, kids are extreme legalists. They want chapter and verse. "Where in the Bible does it say . . . ?" And since it doesn't say, you cannot touch here and there, and because the ministers

never talk about that, kids justify it. We either talk about proper affection over here, or sexual intercourse over there. And most Christian kids are in between. So we talk about the two things that they don't do. They're not into a polite, "Good night, Joe," and they are not into sweet little kisses. But neither are they into sexual intercourse. And the evangelical community has said very little about what is in between.

—Tony Campolo

Helping the *friendless* Kid

Guidelines for helping your least popular kids

When I was in high school,

I was a popular, snobby, social, high school person—"sosh" for short. If the guys didn't wear letterman's jackets or the girls didn't participate in cheer squad, then I wasn't interested in their friendships.

Today I'm not proud of being a sosh. But that was what I was.

I made a commitment to Jesus Christ and His Church as a junior in high school. Immediately I became a Christian sosh. Then one day I had a conversation with a girl not in my social class named Marie. She was a neighbor in the same grade. We had gone through elementary, junior high, and most of high school together, but I never talked with her because she was out—and I was in.

Well, in our conversation Marie told me she had never eaten lunch with anyone from seventh grade to her twelfth-grade year. She was friendless, homely, and unimpressed with me, her "sosh" neighbor. My group of Christian friends began to eat lunch with her. She ended up making a commitment to Christ and then went on to become a youth leader in a Christian youth group.

Until I met Marie I was oblivious to the thousands of kids who are friendless and hurting. Most of the young people in my youth groups have been more like me than Marie. They can't imagine that in every high school in America there are kids who eat lunch alone, walk to school alone, and go home after school and watch TV alone.

BY JIM BURNS

I'm afraid today's teenager is more lonely, desperate, and friendless than ever. I'm also afraid the typical Christian youth group does little to eliminate this problem in our culture.

Sociological Makeup of High Schoolers

To better understand the needs of students we must understand the sociological makeup of the high school campus. High school students today *cluster* together in a small circle of friends. Sociologists tell us that high schoolers tend to have two or three best friends. These friends are usually the most influential people in each other's lives. If the others in Tom's friendship cluster smoke marijuana regularly, then the odds are Tom will take up the habit. If Jenny wears preppie clothes, her friends most likely do also. If Robert attends a youth group regularly, then most likely his best friends attend also. It's within these friendship clusters that peer pressure and peer influence is at its greatest.

How many times have you asked your students, "Why do you do that?" and their reply is "Everybody does!" The everybody they are talking about is their friendship cluster.

We cannot underestimate the value students place on friendships. In *Friendship: A Window on Ministry to Youth*, Donald Posterski reports that in a recent survey on high school students' values, nine out of ten ranked friendships as their highest value.

Peer Ministry

When we understand the sociological makeup of the high schooler, we can then understand the great need in the church today for peer ministry. Ministry to students can best be done by other students. The credibility kids have with other kids makes peer ministry a positive influence in the lives of others.

A good youth ministry today should look for every possible way to include students in leadership and ministry. High school students can take on major responsibilities. They can lead small groups, plan trips, or phone and visit newcomers. Many churches have set up effective peer counseling programs that have become extremely helpful in meeting the ongoing needs of young people.

Helping the Friendless Kid

With this understanding of the sociological makeup of the high schooler and the effectiveness of peer ministry, let's look at some practical ideas on how to work with the "Maries"—the loners and the friendless students—of every group. Here are three practical ideas for helping the friendless kid.

1. Divide your group into small groups.

When your youth group is divided into manageable, small groups, the adult leaders and student leaders can give more attention to individuals in their small groups. You can divide your group up simply for calling one another about activities, or for actual meeting times. Small groups offer intimacy and acceptance.

2. Do service/work projects.

One of the goals of youth ministry should be to break down the caste system (cliques) from the high school campus. One of the best ways to do that is to create service projects where the students from different "castes" need each other. When the "jock" and the "nerd" work side by side at the orphanage, they begin to realize they need each other. They see that their caste system is foolish, and it breaks down.

3. Diversify your program.

Sometimes the friendless students in your group feel friendless because they can't relate to the program. If most of the kids in your group love volleyball and Christian rock music, you must make sure you also plan something for the kid who is a computer wizard and listens to Mozart.

Along with diversifying your program, try to have volunteer adult staff members who relate to kids in all the different caste systems. Don't forget that everyone relates best to people with interests similar to his or her own.

Socialization: A Key to Helping

The bottom line in working with friendless students is to help socialize them into your group. When they become a part of the group and develop meaningful friendships within the group, you can be assured they will remain in the church. Perhaps the greatest spiritual influence is building positive relationships. The friendless kid wants friendships, and you can help make a major difference in his or her life as you provide opportunities for real friendships.

Jim Burns is a youth worker, speaker, and author from Newport Beach, California. He has written several books on youth ministry and leads seminars for youth workers around the country.

Aim

Overview

You'll Need

Growing A Friendship

To help kids practice basic friendship skills: listening and being trustworthy. Key passage: Proverbs 18:24.

Making friends is one of the most important things teenagers do, but it is also one of the most difficult. All teens want friends, yet in each new relationship they attempt, they risk rejection. Defining and practicing two of the basic skills of friendship—trust and communication—will help teens as they nurture old friendships and begin new ones.

1. Trust Me (Games) 10-15 min.
   □ blindfolds (one for every two kids)

2. The Proverbial Friend (Bible study) 15-20 min.
   □ large sheets of paper
   □ magic markers
   □ Bibles
   □ Friendship Puzzles (activity piece A1 from the back of this book)
   □ pencils

3. Let's Hear That Again (Listening exercise) 5 min.
   □ paper
   □ pencils

4. Fantasy Friends (Roleplay) 10-15 min.
   □ Fantasy Friends (activity piece A2)

5. Getting to Know You (Personal interaction) 5 min.

BY PAUL HEIDEBRECHT

1. Trust Me

(Games) 10-15 min.

Playing games in which kids must "blindly" trust others, to learn the place of vulnerability, faith, and communication in friendship. As kids come to the meeting, pass out blindfolds to half of them. Then divide the kids into groups of eight to ten for the first game.

A. Trust Lift

Blindfold one kid in each group, and have him or her lie down on the floor. The person should try to relax while the group slowly lifts him or her in the air, and then lowers him or her back down again. The groups may wish to repeat this several times with different kids blindfolded.

B. Trust Fall

Have the kids form groups of three. One person in each trio should put on a blindfold and stand in front of the other two (facing away from them), with arms extended out sideways. The blindfolded person should then slowly fall backwards (keeping his or her body rigid and feet together). The partners will "catch" the person and ease him or her to the floor. Be sure each kid gets to "fall."

C. Trust Walk

Have the kids form pairs. In each pair, one person should be blindfolded. The other person should then guide him or her safely around the room, helping him or her avoid chairs and other obstacles. Allow only verbal directions (no physical contact). The two should then reverse roles.

After doing these exercises, discuss these questions:
■ **One person in each of these games had to trust others. Why?**
(He or she could not see what was happening, and was vulnerable to being hurt.)
■ **Was it difficult to trust someone else when you had the blindfold on? Why?**
Explain that by entering any relationship, we reveal ourselves and become vulnerable to being hurt or let down.
■ **Why do you trust some people and not others?**
■ **How do good friends earn your trust?**
■ **When you do trust someone, how does it feel?**
■ **During the "Trust Walk," did any of the "seeing" partners find it difficult to explain things to the "blind" person?**
Being able to express yourself and to listen to someone else are key parts of building relationships. Communication fits right in with trust. People will reveal themselves to

2. The Proverbial Friend

(Bible study) 15-20 min.

those whom they trust. They will trust those who really listen to them.

Tell kids that you're now going to look at some expert advice from the Bible on being a trustworthy and attentive friend.

***S**olving friendship dilemmas using advice from Proverbs.* Prior to the meeting, print these seven proverbs on large sheets of paper: Proverbs 17:9, 17; 18:13, 24; 19:7; 27:6, 9. Then hang the printed proverbs on the walls of your meeting room.

Divide the kids into three groups and distribute copies of "Friendship Puzzles" (activity piece A1 from the back of this book) to each person. Assign each group one of the three puzzles. After reading its puzzle, each group should select one or more of the proverbs hanging on the wall to help resolve the problem, and discuss why the proverbs are helpful. Have each group report its findings to the others.

Conclude the study by working with the group to form each of the seven proverbs into a description of a true friend (see examples below). You may want to write the definitions on a chalkboard or large sheet of paper. Here are some sample definitions:

1. Proverbs 17:9: A true friend doesn't gossip about you.
2. Proverbs 17:17: A true friend stays with you even in bad times.
3. Proverbs 18:13: A true friend really listens to you; he or she isn't just waiting for his or her turn to talk.
4. Proverbs 18:24: Having one true friend is better than having lots of shallow friends.
5. Proverbs 19:7: A true friend likes you for who you are, not for your money or possessions.
6. Proverbs 27:6: A true friend tells you the truth even if it hurts.
7. Proverbs 27:9: A true friend is nice to have because he or she advises you and really cares about you.

3. Let's Hear That Again

(Listening Exercise) 5 min.

***P**racticing listening skills in order to understand others better.* Have the kids return to the same groups of three used for "Trust Fall" earlier. In each group, have one kid be the speaker, another the listener, and the third the observer. Then announce a topic. (See suggestions below.) The speaker has three minutes to talk about this subject to the listener while the observer looks on. (The observer may also take notes on the speech.) Then the listener has one minute to repeat in his own words what he heard the speaker say. Finally, the observer has 30 seconds to indicate what the listener missed or misunderstood. How well did he or she really listen? If you want to take the time, repeat this exercise with kids taking different roles. Possible topics:

—how I felt the first day I went to high school

—a problem I had with a family member, and the outcome

—how God answered one of my prayers

—one of my wild, crazy ambitions in life.

Acting out situations in order to apply trust and communication skills. Keep the same trios together, and have them read the two situations presented in "Fantasy Friends" (activity piece A2). Ask groups to complete the story: each person should put himself or herself into a role in the situation and act out what he or she would do.

Note that there is no right or wrong course of action in each scene; you just want kids to have a chance to try out their ideas and practice friendship skills. Give the trios five to seven minutes to work on the first roleplay, then indicate that they should begin the second scene. When time is up, bring everyone back together in a single group.

4. Fantasy Friends

(Roleplay) 10-15 min.

Sharing and praying in pairs. Explain that trust and communication are important in both old relationships and new ones, and that you want to encourage the growth of old and new relationships within this group. To close the meeting, ask the kids to pair up with persons they don't know well. Each should then ask the other one a single question (about school, hobbies, family, etc.) in order to get to know him or her better. These should be questions requiring more than one-word answers!

Allow a couple of minutes for the pairs to talk. Then dismiss the group with prayer, asking God to give them strength to be true friends to others. If your youth are not afraid of praying together, have them pray in the pairs they have formed.

5. Getting to Know You

(Personal Interaction) 5 min.

Dr. Paul Heidebrecht *is Vice-President of Program Development for Christian Service Brigade. He has written and edited lots of youth material.*

□

Aim

Overview

You'll Need

Keeping Friends From Turning to Foes

To demonstrate ways to handle conflicts between friends, and to encourage kids to work at their relationships. Key passage: Ephesians 4:26, 27, 29-32.

There is no escape from conflict, even among the best of friends. The secret to good friendship is knowing how to deal with differences and resolve disagreements. In this meeting, the kids will practice some right and wrong ways to handle conflicts.

1. Getting Punchy (Games) 10 min.
   - ☐ gym mats
   - ☐ three or four bed pillows
   - ☐ dinner bell (or other small bell)

2. I've Got a Problem (Communication exercises) 10-15 min.
   - ☐ I've Got a Problem (activity piece B1 from the back of this book)
   - ☐ pencils

3. Rules for Fighting (Bible study) 10-15 min.
   - ☐ paper
   - ☐ pencils
   - ☐ Bibles

4. You and I (Response exercise) 10-15 min.
   - ☐ Responding "You" or "I" (activity piece B2)
   - ☐ Bibles

5. My Pledge to You (Meditation) 5 min.
   - ☐ index cards   ☐ pencils

*F*ocusing on the topic of conflict and experiencing some of the power of anger. The first game shows put-on, theatrical "anger" and conflict, while the second gets closer to real emotions.

A. Rocky X?

Before the meeting, ask two self-confident guys to come prepared to "fight," costumed as two professional wrestlers (or boxers, karate experts, sumo wrestlers, etc.). You may want to fasten pillows to the front and back of each with belts in order to cushion any "blows." At the meeting, keep the pair out of sight until you announce the fight. Place the mat(s) on the floor as the ring. Divide the other kids into two groups, instructing each group to cheer for one of the contestants. Then introduce the two guys, using wild descriptive adjectives. Grunts, yells, and choreographed punches and falls will make this fun to watch. Ring a bell every 60 seconds to end the round, and after three or five rounds end the fight, declaring a winner or a draw.

B. Pillow Passion

Place a pillow (or several pillows, for a large group) on a table in the front of the room, and have the kids form a line (or lines) and begin filing by. As each person gets to the table, he or she should think about something that makes him or her mad, punch the pillow, and then go back and sit down. Afterwards, ask if all were able to find things they were mad about.

■ **Did it feel good to hit the pillow? If so, why?**

*R*oleplaying potential conflict situations in which kids will recognize both positive and negative ways to respond to each other. Divide the group into pairs. Give each person a copy of "I've Got a Problem" (activity piece B1). One person in each pair should begin as the one with the problem. He or she should expressively read aloud the first statement on the sheet. The partner should then read aloud the five responses (with feeling), pausing after each one so that the person with the problem can indicate if the response was helpful or not. Both should note "helpful" or "not helpful" on their sheets. The two should then reverse roles for the second statement and its responses.

Discuss each of the ten responses briefly.

■ **How did each response make you feel?**
■ **When you have a problem and tell your friend about it, how do you like your friend to respond?**
■ **What happens to friendships when the responses**

1. Getting Punchy

(Games) 10 min.

2. I've Got a Problem

(Exercises)
10-15 min.

3. Rules for Fighting

(Bible study)
10-15 min.

4. You and I

(Response exercise)
10-15 min.

aren't helpful?

Try to get personal examples, if kids are willing to share them. (Have them avoid saying things about other group members.)

*D*iscovering that the Scriptures provide guidelines kids can apply to conflicts in their relationships. Conflict. It even happened in the New Testament church. Paul, the writer of the passage to be studied here, got into a major fight with Peter on one occasion and with his fellow missionary Barnabas on another. These verses on conflict are written by someone who had been through it!

Ask the kids to turn to Ephesians 4:26, 27, 29-32. Distribute paper and pencils. Have kids read the verses and write, in their own words, three guidelines from them that could be helpful. After a few minutes, begin compiling a list of Dos and Don'ts from the guidelines kids found. Sample list:

DO:
Get angry the right way (vs. 25).
Build up others (vs. 29).
Be kind (vs. 32).
Forgive each other (vs. 32).
DON'T:
Hold on to anger (vs. 26).
Talk nastily (vs. 29).
Grieve the Spirit (vs. 30).
Be bitter, malicious (vs. 31).

Anger in this passage is not called a sin—but Paul shows that anger can lead to sin.
■ **How might this happen?**
(Anger can burst out in mean, hurtful words and actions. Or it can lead to resentment and bitterness.)
Next are some positive ways to express negative feelings.

*P*racticing two types of reactions to problems to help kids understand the importance of giving friends the benefit of the doubt in conflict situations. Read I Corinthians 13:7 aloud to the group. Then tell the teens that if they only remember one thing from this meeting, they should remember that love always trusts and hopes in the other person. Love believes the best of others. This kind of trusting love can show in

BY PAUL HEIDEBRECHT

the way we speak to a friend when a problem comes up.

Go over "Responding 'You' or 'I' " (activity piece B2) with your kids, then lead into the following activity.

Divide the kids into two groups, and have each group number themselves from one on up. Then have the first kid from each group come forward. Read one of the "sticky situations" below. Ask one kid to give a negative, accusing response starting with "You . . ." Then have the other respond in a factual and trusting way, beginning with "I . . ." or "I feel . . . when you . . ." The groups may help their representatives come up with responses. When the first pair have finished, go on to the next pair and the next situation. Here are some suggested problems for them to respond to.

Sticky situations:

- Your friend doesn't pick you for his/her team in gym.
- Your friend borrows an album of yours and scratches it.
- Your friend only seems to talk to you when he/she needs help with homework.
- Your friend spends all his/her time with a new "sweetheart."
- Your friend picks another person to be his/her roommate on the upcoming choir tour.
- Your friend asks your advice about a family problem, but then does the opposite of what you suggest.
- Fellow swim team members criticize your performance at a meet, and your friend stands by and says nothing.

*P*ledging to try to improve a particular friendship. Distribute index cards. Ask kids to think of one friendship that they consider important, but that needs to be improved. Have each youth write a pledge on the card, addressed to the friend ("I pledge to you, Debbie"), or to God, in the form of prayer if they like. Explain that this card is only for their own use; they don't actually have to give it to the friend. Kids should indicate what they will do to handle their side of the conflict in a better way. Encourage them to be very specific. The cards should be kept private. Conclude the meeting with prayer.

5. My Pledge To You

(Personal meditation) 5 min.

Dr. Paul Heidebrecht *is Vice-President of Program Development for Christian Service Brigade. He has written and edited lots of youth material.*

□

Aim

Overview

You'll Need

Overcoming Obstacles

To help kids recognize and deal with common obstacles to positive friendships.

Friendships are extremely important to kids today. So building good friendships has never been more important. But most kids run into problems in friendships that sometimes stop the friendships cold. Through the activities of this meeting, help your kids recognize some of the obstacles they come up against and learn how to deal with them.

1. **To Take a Stand** (Action discussion) 10-15 min.
   - ☐ five large sheets of paper   ☐ marker

2. **Obvious Obstacles** (Brainstorming) 10 min.
   - ☐ chalkboard and chalk or newsprint and marker

3. **Proverbial Friendship** (Proverb game) 10-15 min.
   - ☐ Overcoming Proverbs (activity piece C1 from the back of this book)
   - ☐ Bibles

4. **Love That Overcomes** (Bible study) 10-15 min.
   - ☐ Friends in Love (activity piece C2)
   - ☐ pencils   ☐ Bibles

5. **Friendship Goals** (Writing goals) 5 min.
   - ☐ note cards or small pieces of paper
   - ☐ pencils

BY JIM BURNS

Discovering that obstacles can hamper good friendships. Before your meeting, write the following words on five separate large sheets of paper and post them in different sections of the room so that kids can stand under them.

Strongly Agree
Agree
Not Sure
Disagree
Strongly Disagree

As your meeting starts, read the statements below and have each student stand under the sign that best describes his or her belief about the statement. Have kids think about the statement and decide where they are going to stand before you let them move. Discuss each statement as kids are standing under different words.

1. Friends have a big influence on my life.
2. It's easy to make good friends.
3. God doesn't care who my friends are.
4. If I have problems in a friendship, it's best to drop the friendship.
5. The kind of friend I am is important in developing a good friendship.

This discussion should bring out that there *are* obstacles to good friendships. Let kids know that you're going to be looking at some of those obstacles and how to get around them.

Brainstorming obstacles to good friendships. Ask your kids to list as many obstacles to a positive friendship they can think of. Write every answer kids give on the chalkboard, overhead, or newsprint. In brainstorming, any answer is okay. Encourage kids to share anything that comes to their minds. Below are a few of the obstacles they might come up with. You might have to give them one or two to get them started.
—differing backgrounds
—differing interests
—jealousy, envy
—pride
—insensitivity

1. To Take A Stand

(Action discussion)
10-15 min.

2. Obvious Obstacles

(Brainstorming) 10 min.

3. Proverbial Friendship

(Proverb game) 10-15 min.

4. Love That Overcomes

(Bible study) 10-15 min.

5. Friendship Goals

(Writing goals) 5 min.

When kids are finished, have your class discuss *how* these obstacles can hinder good friendships. Pick out four or five from the list to discuss. Then have kids offer ways that any of the other obstacles can hinder friendships.

Discovering Biblical solutions to friendship problems. **The Bible is filled with important advice on overcoming obstacles to friendship. The Book of Proverbs is especially helpful, and the advice given thousands of years ago is just as pertinent today.**

Have ''Overcoming Proverbs'' (activity piece C1 from the back of this book) cut apart ahead of time as indicated on the sheet. Pass out one proverb half to each of your kids. If you have more kids than proverb halves, give out as many duplicate copies as needed so that everyone has one. Then have each find the person with the other half of the same proverb. If they aren't sure their combinations are right, have kids check the Bible. When they've found each other, have each pair discuss the verse and how it applies to overcoming obstacles in friendships today.

After a few minutes of discussion, have each pair report briefly on what they discovered.

Examining the characteristics of love. **We've seen some principles that help overcome obstacles to good friendship. But there's one principle that Jesus talked about a lot that can overcome almost any problem in a friendship: love. I Corinthians 13 is the apostle Paul's definition of love.**

Have your students read I Corinthians 13:4-7 and fill in ''Friends in Love'' (activity piece C2).

When kids are finished, have volunteers share some of what they've written.

Setting goals for overcoming obstacles to positive friendships. Give kids pencils and note cards or small sheets of paper. Let them know they are going to do three things on this card. First, have kids write the names of three people with whom they would like to become better friends. Second, next to each name, have them write down one obstacle they might have to overcome to be better friends with this person. Third, they should write down one principle characteristic of love and how it can help them get past that obstacle.

Encourage kids to take action on overcoming obstacles in their friendships by practicing real love.

Jim Burns is a youth worker, speaker, and author from Newport Beach, California. He has written several books on youth ministry and leads seminars for youth workers around the country.

Aim

Overview

You'll Need

Peer Pressure at School

To help kids recognize and work through the challenges of peer pressure by relying on God's power and presence.

Peer pressure is a reality that no student can be ordered to ignore. It is the pressure to conform to other people's standards even when they are different from the student's own. This pressure can have positive or negative results. Negative peer pressure, unfortunately, pervades every area of kids' lives. This session will help kids discover that God's promises are truthful and lead to an abundant life.

1. **When Push Comes to Shove** (Skit and discussion) 10-15 min.

   □ A Little Heavenly Pressure (activity piece D1 from the back of this book)
   □ chalkboard, newsprint
   □ note cards, pencils

2. **It's Always Been Around** (Skits and practice) 15-20 min.

   □ Bibles
   □ note cards from earlier, pencils

3. **Pressure and Promises** (Bible study) 15-20 min.

   □ Pressure Versus Promises (activity piece D2)
   □ note cards from earlier, pencils
   □ Bibles
   □ prizes (optional)

4. **You've Got a Friend** (Prayer writing) 5 min.

   □ Bible
   □ note cards from earlier, pencils

BY BILL REIF

*A*dmitting that peer pressure is real and that many of our day-to-day decisions are influenced by it. To get started, have two creative kids act out the short skit, "A Little Heavenly Pressure" (activity piece D1 from the back of this book). On a chalkboard or newsprint, gather responses to the following questions:

■ **How would you define peer pressure?**

(Feeling the pressure to do something simply to gain the approval of others.)

■ **What are some things our friends ask us to do, or we feel we need to do, to gain their approval?**

Answers will vary, but be aware that attitudes are formed as much by peer pressure as actions are.

■ **Why do we sometimes go along with, or give in, to peer pressure?**

Have each student write his or her single greatest area of personal struggle with peer pressure on a note card. Have kids keep their cards hidden.

As much as we hate to admit it, peer pressure is real in our lives and does have an effect on us. But we're going to discover that—despite what you might think— peer pressure has always been around.

*C*reating skits to show that even people in the Bible had to face pressure and learn to say no. **We might not often think about it in this way, but some of the great people in the Bible struggled with, and even gave in, to peer pressure.**

Divide the kids into three groups. Have each group study one of the following stories:

Peter's denial (Mt. 26:69-75)
Aaron and the golden calf (Ex. 32:1-6, 17-24)
Saul and the Amalekites (I Sam. 15:1-3, 12-23)

Have groups create short skits that act out the events of their stories. But have each group create a new ending in which the principal character stands up to peer pressure instead of giving in to it. Give kids about ten minutes to create their scenes, then pull everyone together for a performance of each skit. After each scene, discuss the following questions:

■ What part did peer pressure play in the story?

■ Why was it hard for the main character to say no to peer pressure?

■ What was the price for saying no?

1. When Push Comes to Shove

(Skit and discussion) 10-15 min.

2. It's Always Been Around

(Skits and practice) 15-20 min.

At the conclusion of all three skits, point out that the major challenge of peer pressure is saying no to people you're afraid won't like you unless you say yes. We become so used to saying yes to other people, and no to Jesus, that some of us have almost lost the ability to say no to our friends when we need to. Tell kids that you want to help them practice saying no by having them respond with bold "no's" to these questions and statements:

—Since your parents are out of town, let's have a major party at your house tonight.

—How about just you and me and one bottle?

—Drinking really doesn't affect my driving, so you can ride with me.

—I'm not going to gossip. Come on, tell me what she said.

—If I guess it, will you tell me if I'm right?

—(Guy to gal) If you really loved me, you'd want to.

—(Guy to gal) But it's all right because I really love you.

—(Gal to guy) My parents are out for the night. I wouldn't mind if you wanted to stay here, just to keep me company.

—(Gal to guy) But my parents said it would be all right to have a friend stay over.

—I'm going to bomb that biology test tomorrow. Unless you could give me the answers after you take it?

If only saying no were really that easy! Let's see what faith really is so we can believe more in God's promises than in the promises of our friends.

*D*iscovering the difference between responses of faith and reactions to peer pressure. Read Hebrews 11:1.

■ **How would you define faith?**

Help kids understand that Biblical faith is believing that what God says is true and will come to pass, whether or not immediate circumstances make it seem true. Point out that giving in to peer pressure is exactly the opposite, because it means believing only what other people and circumstances seem to make true.

Divide the kids into small groups (three to six kids) making sure each group has pencils. Pass out "Pressure Versus Promises" (activity piece D2). Quickly read through the instructions and answer any questions. Tell kids to pick five of the examples from the list and come up with pressure situations as fast as they can. You might give prizes (joke or serious) for the first group. Have the groups share some of

3. Pressure And Promises

(Bible study) 15-20 min.

their answers. Then discuss the following questions.

■ **What did this exercise tell us about peer pressure and God's promises?**

Help kids see that obeying God's commands *may* force them to go against the flow of their culture. But also point out that if we obey God's commands, by faith, they will always lead to the promise of God's reward.

■ **Does peer pressure sometimes have rewards, too?**

■ **What are some of those rewards? Are they short-term or long-term rewards?**

■ **Are God's rewards short or long term?**

Have your kids write on their note cards any promise from God that might apply in the long run if they resist pressure in the area they wrote down earlier.

*H*elping kids see Jesus as the One who identifies with their pressures and will come alongside to help. Read Hebrews 2:17, 18. Point out that Jesus was made like us in order to be able to completely help us in times of pressure.

■ **Do you think Jesus identifies with you in times of intense peer pressure? Why or why not?**

Kids should see that Christ knew pressure like everyone else. He was pressured by the crowds, by the Pharisees, by His own family, even by the disciples.

■ **Would it be a help to have a friend like Jesus to stand with you in times of peer pressure?**

Have kids use the backs of their note cards to write notes to Jesus. Not to some faraway Jesus up in Heaven, but to the Jesus who stands with them every day at school. Have kids ask for His help as they decide to stand against the particular area of peer pressure they have listed on their cards. Ask kids to keep their cards and to look at what they wrote every morning this week before school.

Close with a prayer for strength and remind kids that you are available to help with particular and persistent areas of defeat.

Bill Reif is an exciting youth speaker and writer from Alabama. Formerly a youth pastor, Bill now spends much of his time speaking to young people and their leaders.

□

4. You've Got A Friend

(Prayer writing) 5 min.

Aim

Overview

You'll Need

Can Anything Good Come from Cliques?

To guide kids' thinking about the beneficial and devastating aspects of cliques; to help them imagine how God might use social relationships in positive ways. Key passage: Luke 6:31-36.

Kids—not unlike adults—have a strong need to be accepted, to belong. Every day they are faced with cliques, which either provide or deprive them of that acceptance. This meeting examines cliques: whom they benefit and victimize, which ones are common, and why they form. Then it looks at what the Bible says about accepting others and encourages kids to explore ways of making their group more inclusive.

1. Cliques Are Everywhere (Reading) 20-25 min.

   ☐ *Star-Bellied Sneetches* by Dr. Seuss
   ☐ rocking chair or other props for the reading
   ☐ optional: *Sneetches* film, projector, screen
   ☐ "Stuck Inside" (activity piece E1 from the back of this book)

2. Cliques on Campus (Rate-a-clique) 10-15 min.

   ☐ chalkboard and chalk or poster board and markers
   ☐ paper (ballots) and pencils

3. The Unclique (Posters) 15-20 min.
   ☐ Bibles
   ☐ poster board
   ☐ markers

BY JIM HANCOCK

1. Cliques Are Everywhere!

(Reading) 20-25 min.

Reading and discussing a story or poem that deals with cliques. **Everyone is affected by cliques— some people as beneficiaries, others as victims.**

■ **What are the benefits of a clique (if you're on the inside)?**

■ **In what ways (actual and imagined) are people victimized by cliques?**

■ **Have you ever been victimized by a clique? What was that like?**

The beneficiaries of a clique are its insiders—people who are accepted because, by the standards of the clique, they are acceptable. And the outsiders are outside because, for reasons known in the clique, they don't measure up. It's simple, actually: some people rate and some don't. It's just that way. Or is it?

Do one (or both if you have the time) of the following dramatic readings.

Reading 1:

Why do some people rate when others don't? No one has put it better than Dr. Theodore Geisel in his treatise (dramatic pause), ***Star-Bellied Sneetches.***

Read Dr. Seuss's *Sneetches* book here, or have someone read it for you. Milk it! Pitch in a rocking chair or other props if you want. By all means make it a production. By having some fun with the reading you'll free anybody who might be tempted to hold back because it's a children's book. Or, you may want to see if your public library has a copy of the film on hand.

■ **What do you like best about this story?**

■ **What is the real conflict among the Sneetches?**

■ **Do you see any parallels to life in senior high?**

■ **What solutions does this story suggest?**

Problem cliques reveal people with problems. After we've thought for a few minutes about cliques at school, we'll come back to the problems that produce cliques.

Reading 2:

Turn to "Stuck Inside" (activity piece E1).

Here's a reading by Steve Lawhead from *Campus Life* magazine. It's called "Stuck Inside." Listen carefully.

You'll want to read this with lots of "oomph." "Stuck Inside" carries lots of power in a few words.

(Option: you may want to have one, or better yet, several, kids read it.)

■ **What elements from your life in high school can you**

2. Cliques On Campus

(Rate-a-clique)
10-15 min.

identify in this reading?
- **What is the writer feeling? What are the clues that reveal those emotions?**
- **Is there a victim in the library scene? Who? Why?**
- **How would you describe the motives of the writer? Why?**
- **What is the writer struggling with as the reading ends? Is that a realistic struggle?**
- **If the writer asked you for advice, what would you say?**

Identifying common groups at the kids' high schools and rating which groups are the most and least important. **People group together everywhere. That's part of being human. Don't let the exceptions spoil your understanding of the rule. There *are* hermits, and some people *do* like to sit alone on buses or prefer the company of books to that of people. But most of us see ourselves in relation to other humans. Our picture of those associations may be competitive—even combative—but more often they are in some measure dependent, and in the best cases, interdependent.**
- **What is the difference between dependence and interdependence?**

(Dependence is one sided. Interdependence means there is give and take, with both people helping each other, and both leaning on each other.)
- **Why is interdependence better?**
- **Do you think of cliques as typically dependent or interdependent?**

Have students brainstorm as many groups that exist at their schools as possible. Make a list of them on a chalkboard or piece of poster board. Have kids include the "staging area" on campus where individuals go to be identified with these groups. (Where, for example, do band members tend to gather? Is there a smoking area? Do the jocks congregate in one area or by teams? Where would you go to find the drama students? And so on.)

Next, pass out paper and pencils. Have each kid pick the group he or she finds most open (to admitting new members and interacting with people outside the group) and least open. Have the kids write the names of those groups. Have two kids collect the ballots and tally the results. Is there a consensus? Which groups were voted most open? Which least open? Have kids discuss their choices.

3. The Unclique

(Posters) 15-20 min.

*M*aking posters that explore how the group can become more Biblically inclusive. **There's plenty of evidence that people form cliques as a security measure. They feel unsafe and insecure in the high school environment—just like the rest of us. The fear of failure and of looking foolish is something a lot of us wake up with every morning.**

In that atmosphere it's pretty natural to seek the safety of friendships. Most cliques aren't exclusive out of a desire to hurt anyone. People get into cliques to protect themselves from being hurt.

But what if a clique was formed with the specific purpose of being inclusive, of letting everyone in, instead of keeping some people out? Could it work?

(Admittedly, this contradicts the definition of clique, but the contradiction illustrates an interesting point.)

■ **Have you ever seen a truly inclusive clique? What was it like?**

■ **What kind of attitude would you have to have to develop an inclusive clique? How would the fear and insecurity that drive us into cliques affect the establishment of such a group?**

Have students divide into three or four groups to work together for about ten minutes. Have each group read Luke 6:31-36 and discuss the following questions:

■ What do these words from Jesus tell us about being inclusive?

■ What would our group have to do in order to become more inclusive? What would it look like? What would it cost us? What would we get in return?

Next, using the poster board, have each group make an advertisement that describes the inclusiveness of the youth group and invites others to join it. Then have each group briefly share its advertisement with the rest of the group.

Close with prayer asking God to help the group members (including yourself) become less afraid for themselves and more open to each other.

Jim Hancock *is director of youth ministries at Solana Beach Presbyterian Church, Solana Beach, California. He contributes regularly to* Youthworker *and* Group, *and leads seminars at the National Youth Workers' Convention.*

1

Friendship Challenge

In a major survey, one out of five high school students said they felt worthless, self-critical, and lonely. Most who felt this way said that outside of their families, they had no group of friends that they belonged to. Some had thoughts of committing suicide because they were so unhappy. Make a friendship poster challenging kids to make at least five friendly gestures to people they usually do not befriend during the week. Explain that at the next meeting, you will discuss ways you reached out and how kids responded.

2

Measure My Friendship?

Have kids measure their friendship maturity. Results are for their eyes alone. After the self-test, discuss statements with the group. Which habits build friendships? Which ones destroy them?

Decide if you have these attitudes and actions never, sometimes, often, or always.
1. I like myself as a person.
2. I put people down.
3. I strike up conversations with people I don't know.
4. I try to beat out people in sports, academics, etc.
5. I learn the names and interests of new kids.
6. I ask people I know to join me in various activities.
7. I get mad if friends talk about their achievements.
8. I invite kids to my home.
9. I listen to kids' problems.
10. I get jealous of other people that my friends like.
11. I offer my help when a friend is in need.
12. I encourage kids who are discouraged.
13. I don't like it when a friend has different ideas from mine.
14. I like to share my feelings with kids I trust.
15. I forgive and forget if a friend hurts me.

BY ELAINE McCALLA
With Lucy Townsend

3

What Size Friendship?

Divide kids into teams. Explain that reaching out to people involves personal effort. We might compare that effort to sweaters that come in different sizes: small, medium, and large. Small-sized reaching out might mean smiling at a person or saying hello. Medium-sized reaching out might involve listening to a person's problem. Large-sized reaching out could mean taking care of a family's children for several weeks. Give each team two minutes to think of the small-, medium-, or large-sized acts of friendship it has experienced. The group with the most answers wins the game.

4
Wacky Activities

Divide kids into groups of three to four people and put their names and telephone numbers on a bulletin board. Each mini-group decides on one or more social activities (the wackier, the better) the group can do in the next month. For example, kids might meet in the park at dawn to sail toy sailboats. On the bulletin board, list scheduled activities beside each group. Once a month, have kids evaluate their activities. Were they fun? Did kids get to know each other better? For several months "round robin" the teens so that different kids are in each group.

5
Tiny Friends

Usually the children in church admire teens and try to imitate them. Encourage your teens to make friends with younger kids. They might make an effort to learn younger children's names, speak to them in the halls, or possibly even help out with a Sunday school class, club, or baseball team.

6

Friendship Poll

Have kids take a poll at your church or in a shopping mall. Kids are to ask people of all ages to name the three most important ingredients of friendship. Kids might award those who participate in the poll with red heart stickers. Have kids combine results and discuss the top ten. Compare the public's opinions with those of the youth group. Publish results in the church newsletter.

Illustration by Donna Nelson

7
The Friendly Kidnappers

Here's an unusual way to help new kids feel welcome in your youth group. Have some friendly long-time youth group members kidnap the newest members for an early morning breakfast. Have teens notify parents ahead of time, but "Mum's the word." Parents are not to awaken their teen. When the old-timers arrive for the kidnapping, the victims are allowed no more than 15 minutes to get ready. Over breakfast, old-timers must share with the newest member a childhood antic they were punished for, an antic they got away with, and one of their happiest memories.

8
Let 'Em Know

Have your kids ever thought of sharing how much they care about another person? Maybe a Sunday school teacher or youth leader has really helped them, or maybe a church usher or janitor goes out of his way to make them welcome. Encourage kids to put an ad in the newspaper telling that special someone how great he or she is. Or instead of the usual T-P party, teens might tie yellow ribbons around anything growing in the special person's yard. How about a ''You're Special'' sign mysteriously planted under a bedroom window? Or maybe kids would enjoy a moonlight serenade.

9
Friendship Builders

Have each teen bring to the meeting something to represent a hobby or special interest (tennis racket, snapshots, football, hiking boot, etc.). Hand out the following questions, and ask kids to circle questions they would most like to be asked about their hobby. Then pair up kids and have them question each other. Remind kids that in conversation, both people need to offer some information about themselves or give an opinion.
1. How long have you been interested in this?
2. What kinds of materials or equipment do you like to use?
3. What turns you on about this activity?
4. Do you get paid for it?
5. Do you plan to make this into a career?
6. What talents or skills do you need to do this?
7. Are there others who do this, too?
8. Where do you get your ideas?
9. Do you think you'll ever lose interest in this?
10. What is your greatest achievement, the one that makes you the most proud?

Questions based on those formulated by Dr. Barbara B. Varenhorst in *Real Friends* (San Francisco: Harper & Row, Publishers, 1983), p. 47.

10
Friend Hunt

Arrange with another youth group to ''find a friend'' in a shopping mall. Here's how it works. One group meets at one end of the mall; the other group meets at the opposite end. In one of the groups, take an instant-print photo of each person—from the neck up—so clothes won't be a giveaway. Give each photo to one of the kids from the other group. The hunt begins! Each person with a photo tries to find his or her pictured ''friend.'' To keep things moving, don't let the hunted kids stay in any one store for more than one minute. When someone finds his victim, he or she initiates a five-W's conversation (see the activity by that name).

11
Feelings

Divide kids into groups and explain that you will give a typical social situation like, "When I try out for a team, I feel . . ." Each team will complete the sentence with a feeling word like "excited," and then think of an analogy using animals or something else from nature. "As excited as an alligator chasing after a duck." Teams have two minutes to write down as many analogies as they can think of. When time is called, each team will receive a point for each unique analogy, that is, an analogy that is not found on another team's list. Sample starters: On my first day of school, I feel . . .
When a friend invites me to a party, I feel . . .

12
Friendship Tips

Have kids make up some wise rules. Read Proverbs 19:1 ("Better a poor man whose walk is blameless than a fool whose lips are perverse," NIV); the rule might be "In choosing friends, it is better to select a poor, honest person than a rich liar." Divide kids into groups and have each group make up a rule based on a Biblical passage. Verses: Proverbs 3:31, 32; 6:23-26; 11:13; 11:16; 13:10; 13:20; 14:7; 22:24.

13
Postage Stamp Friends

Provide kids with envelopes, stamps, magazines, scissors, and have them design a cheery card to a friend. If they can't think of anyone to write, have them send a card to an older teen or adult who has helped or inspired them.

14
The Five W'S

Give your kids some help in starting conversations with strangers. Write the five W's on the chalkboard and give some possible questions kids might ask:
Who—"I'm _____ , WHO are you?"
What—"WHAT'S that?" (Ask what the person is doing.)
When—"WHEN did you get here?"
Where—"WHERE are you from? I'm from _____ ."
Why—"WHY did you decide to come to our church?"

Have kids practice a five-W's conversation by pairing up with someone in the room they don't know well. After five minutes, switch roles.

15
TV Friends

Play an icebreaker game called "Famous TV Friends." Make up cards with names of famous TV friends (LaVerne & Shirley, Scarecrow & Mrs. King, Cagney & Lacey, the Simon brothers, Michael Knight & KITT, etc.). When all kids arrive, tape a card to the back of each person. Divide the group into pairs and explain that at the signal, kids will have five minutes to ask their partners questions about the famous TV friends on their backs, but each partner may give only a yes or no answer. When time is called, each person will guess the names of the friends on his back. If both members of the pair have correct answers, they can give each other a friendly hug.

16
Friendship Olympics

Divide kids into teams and give each team a score card listing the important qualities of friendship: loyalty, trust, communication, acceptance, sharing, cooperation. Then plan events to test each team's ability in these areas. Sample events:

1. Cooperation. See which team can climb, jump, or somehow get over a volleyball net in the best time.

2. Sharing. See which team can build the highest free-standing tower using four sheets of paper and 12 paper clips.

3. Communication. Name each team a specific animal (cat, dog, pig, duck, etc.) and then tell everybody to mix with others as much as they can. Call "Freeze!", turn out the lights, and tell kids to find everyone in their team by making the animal sounds. After one or two minutes, turn on the lights. Give points according to how many animals have found each other.

4. Trust. Have kids share in teams an embarrassing event. Ask teams to tell the best story of their group (without giving names). Then have kids judge the amount of trust needed to tell that story.

17
Be A True Friend

Read aloud I Corinthians 13:4-7 and have kids follow along in their Bibles. The second time replace the word *love* with the words *a loving friend*. Help kids recall ways they and their friends have shown love for each other. On the chalkboard, have kids list the expressions of love described in the passage (*is patient, is kind, does not envy, is not self-seeking,* etc.). Put students in pairs, and assign each pair a loving act (for example, *is patient*). Pairs must think of a time when either they or a friend expressed that kind of love. Afterward, have volunteers give an example of each loving trait in action.

18
My Friends

Have kids write the characteristics of two fictional teens: the ideal friend and the teen to avoid at all costs. After kids have written descriptions, list their answers on the board. Explain that their preferences determine the kinds of people they attract and avoid. Have kids privately list four or five friends they have had. Then have them write three or four qualities that characterize each friend. Include both negative and positive attributes. These should not be shown to anyone. Ask if kids see a pattern in the qualities they have listed about their friends. Explain that through making friends, kids can discover what they like and value.

19
Craft & Friendship Fair

Invite an adult class (or the whole church) to a Craft & Friendship Fair. Everyone who comes should be prepared to share some skill, craft, sport or hobby. Teens can set up tables and provide refreshments. If kids feel awkward about initiating questions, have them go over the Friendship Builders' questions (see the activity by that name). Because it is easier to remember names if they can be associated with faces, take instant-print photographs and display them on a bulletin board. Label each photograph with names of persons pictured. Encourage kids to make at least one new friend by the end of the fair.

Elaine McCalla *is a free-lance writer and teacher from Livonia, Michigan. She has taught junior high and high school and now teaches math at Henry Ford Community College.*

Dr. Lucy Townsend *is a free-lance editor from Elgin, Illinois, and has edited a series of drama books.*

20
Dear Blabby

Divide kids into groups of three, and write and answer Dear Blabby letters. Letters should express a problem they have or someone they know has had with a friend. Here's a sample:

Dear Blabby,

My friend Susie and I had an argument last week, and I haven't heard from her since. I think she was at fault, so she should apologize to me, but she won't. How can I make her realize my point of view? I still want to be her friend.

Lonely

Have kids exchange letters with another group and write answers. Then have each group present questions and their answers.

Evaluating And Closing A GROUP

When should you end a group?
How can you make the good-byes good?

BY GARY W. DOWNING

"Old groups never die, they just smell that way!" The experience of being in a group that just fades away or hangs on interminably is a rotten one. There is a sense of failure or a feeling of boredom that can taint one's overall recollection of a group experience. Most groups last either too short or too long a time. How do you as a leader find the balance?

Evaluating

Evaluation is a crucial key to group health. Too often we assume that "no news is good news." We think we'll hear when things aren't right, because people are prone to criticize so quickly. Not true, and we also miss the affirmation an evaluation process can offer.

Evaluation is a negative word connoting school report cards or bad performance reviews. What it ought to mean is a positive opportunity for taking the pulse of a group so the group can better respond to the changes that have occurred since it began. "How are we doing?" is a question that will help a group feel good about itself and become more effective in the long run.

It is best to set up a formal evaluation process at the beginning of a group experience. For example, "Let's commit ourselves to five more weekly meetings together and then check signals." Or "When a year is complete, why not assume our group is closed down until we determine a new direction?" These are ways of setting a formal time limit for a group so evaluation is built in.

The length of time before you evaluate a group depends on many factors, like the scope of the curriculum, or the project or station in life that has brought the group together. Six weeks, six months, a year, etc., can best be determined by the natural flow of a group. Ask the group to decide when those points of evaluation should occur. They become part of the covenant or agreement that clarifies what a member's commitment should be.

There is also a natural, informal process of evaluation that goes on constantly in a group. It occurs every time a member has to decide if he or she will come to a scheduled gathering, or go along with an activity in which a group is engaged. "What's happening?" or "How are you feeling?" are questions you can ask along the way to get a reading on people's evaluation of the group experience.

I watched a friend who is normally very outgoing and talkative withdraw and remain very quiet during our Bible study. I wondered if he were having trouble with our group, or if something else were going on in his life. At the end of the meeting, I approached him and said, "You were pretty quiet today. I'm a little concerned about how you're feeling." I discovered that he was deeply troubled by a personal problem that had nothing to do with the group.

A couple of weeks later, another member appeared sullen and remained silent for the entire Bible study and discussion. When I called him on the phone later that day, he acknowledged that he hadn't prepared for the lesson, was tired, and was turned off by another member who was "hogging the air waves" with a series of mini-speeches that had little to do with the purpose of the group.

Each situation provided an opportunity for a personal contact and a chance to gain some informal evaluation of the group experience. If I had waited until the formal time for group evaluation, those friends would probably have dropped out because their needs and expectations weren't being met. Part of the role of being a facilitative leader in a group is to have our ears tuned to what people are saying along the way in order to fine tune the group. It requires sensitivity and openness to the signals members will offer—often nonverbally.

Closing

There are times when a group should terminate. Either by initial design, or by the development of factors unforeseen at the group's inception, sometimes it is in the best interests of the members for the group to come to closure.

It's hard to determine with certainty when the termination of a group should occur. It's helpful if the process has been set initially. But whether the group ends by design or default, one of the important roles of a leader is to help a group die.

The end of a group should have two characteristics:

■ **Celebration** for the experience. Time spent with a group of people should not be lightly dismissed, for no participant is the same as when he or she began. The changes that have occurred over the life of the group can be recounted, acknowledged, and affirmed. Regardless of what has been accomplished, relationships have been changed and members are in a different place than when they began. Let's celebrate those changes and thank God for them!

■ **Recollection** is another characteristic that should mark the closing of a group. In light of the experiences each member has had, what can be remembered and brought to the rest of their lives? Memories are an important part of the legacy of a group. They

represent one way of furthering the effect of the group. Whether by writing a report, planning a reunion, or taking time for closing testimonials, it is valuable for members of a group to reflect on what they have felt, learned, and accomplished together.

People go through a grief process of sorts when a group ends. If the group experience has been positive, in the euphoria of a celebration, the leader may be tempted to continue the group, when to do so isn't healthy. One way of dealing with a group member who says, "Isn't that great! We should keep meeting!" is to say, "Yes, it has been good. Let's meet in a couple of weeks to see what kind of directions *people from this group* might pursue together." Or, you might encourage that person to give leadership to a new group of his or her friends who might be interested. Sometimes a group can reproduce the positive parts of its experience with other people in new settings.

Every group has an end. Wouldn't it be great if your group could end on the note that Jesus gave His friends, "My peace I leave with you . . ." Jesus in His human form had to leave His disciples. But they were able to celebrate the love He gave them and to recollect the experiences they shared together. Now the impact of their experience is ours to have, to hold, and to give away. We are that group's living legacy.

Sample Evaluation Sheet

Have members circle one ending to each statement.
A. How I Feel About the Group
1. I feel I know most of the other members: (a) fairly well (b) a little bit (c) hardly at all.

2. Communication in the group was: (a) very open (b) so-so (c) closed.
3. My personal involvement in the group was: (a) high (b) okay (c) low.
B. How I Feel About the Content We Discussed
1. I felt the topics were: (a) right on target (b) fairly helpful (c) irrelevant.
2. I understood what was being covered: (a) completely (b) pretty well (c) hardly at all.
3. I came to the group prepared: (a) most of the time (b) sometimes (c) rarely.
C. How I Feel About What We Accomplished
1. I felt the group: (a) got a lot done (b) loafed a little (c) avoided its task.
2. I feel this group: (a) was very helpful to me (b) helped me a little (c) wasn't helpful.
3. Overall, I felt my experience in this group was: (a) growth inspiring (b) neutral (c) harmful to me.
D. How I Feel About the Leadership in Our Group
1. The style of leadership was: (a) warm and open (b) dominated by a group (c) dominated by one person.
2. I feel the leaders: (a) really understood me (b) sometimes understood me (c) misunderstood me.
3. I feel the leaders: (a) really cared for me (b) were generally genuine (c) seemed closed.
E. What Suggestions I Would Offer to Improve the Group:

☐

Dr. Gary W. Downing is executive minister of the Colonial Church of Edina, Minnesota. Formerly he was executive director for Youth Leadership and was part of the National Training Staff for Young Life.

BY THE H. G. PLAYERS

Class Clones

A Revealing Skit on Peer Pressure

Characters:

TED—an excitable nerd

SHEILA—a scatterbrained

cheerleader type

RUSSELL—a likable hoodlum

MR. WHITAKER—the teacher

Other kids without speaking parts

Scene One

A high school classroom. Mr. Whitaker is at his desk at the front of the room, grading history papers. Ted, Sheila, and Russell are seated near one another, with other kids seated behind them.

TED: Pssst! Going to the game tonight, Sheila?

SHEILA: Am I going? What kind of question is that? Of course I'm going. If our team wins tonight's game that means they go on to the conference play-offs! I wouldn't miss it for the world.

TED: How about you, Russell? I don't suppose you're interested in such things as basketball.

RUSSELL: How right you are, my friend Ted the Nerd. At the very bottom of my list of things to worry about are—in descending order—basketball and history.

SHEILA: I wish I didn't have to worry about history. If I didn't pass yesterday's test, I may flunk this quarter. My parents will kill me.

TED: It did seem like that test was a little tougher than usual.

RUSSELL: I didn't notice. Ah, well, if I flunk, it won't be the first time. Nor will it be the last.

TED: One of these days it WILL be the last time for you, Russell, because they'll be throwing you out of school for good.

MR. WHITAKER (*finally finished with the papers, looks up*): Well, students, I've got some good news . . . and some bad news. (*Stands up to pass out papers.*)

RUSSELL: Tell us the bad news first.

Illustration by Donna Nelson

MR. WHITAKER: Russell, I'm afraid you're going to find both bits of news bad. First of all, for the first time in recent memory, my entire history class managed to fail a history exam. *(All students groan.)*

SHEILA: I'm dead.

TED: Me, too.

MR. WHITAKER: Ah, but luckily for you all—and this is the good news—I'm giving you a second chance to pass the same test. *(Starts handing back papers.)*

RUSSELL: You're right. Both are equally bad.

TED: Excuse me, sir, but you said we're going to have another chance on this test. Does that mean tomorrow?

MR. WHITAKER: As a matter of fact, Mr. Thompson, it does. *(Hands paper to Ted.)* I'd like to squeeze this test in before the weekend, and since tomorrow is Friday, we'll have to have our test then.

SHEILA: But Mr. Whitaker, sir, tonight's the big game. You can't expect us to stay home and study for a history test when our team is on the verge of making the conference play-offs!

MR. WHITAKER: I don't know anything about conference play-offs. And it is beyond me why they would schedule a basketball game on a school night. But I'm sure you'll all find some time to study.

SHEILA: We could wait until next week to take the test again.

MR. WHITAKER: Sorry, Sheila. It'll have to be tomorrow.

SHEILA: But why?

MR. WHITAKER: Suffice it to say that when *you* look bad, *I* look bad. And I don't want to look bad. Now I'd advise you all to use these last few minutes to get in a little studying. Judging from these papers, you can use all the studying you can get. See you tomorrow. *(Exits.)*

SHEILA: If I flunk that test, I'll never pass this class. But if I stay home to study tonight, I'll miss the biggest game of the year!

TED: He's just doing his job, I guess.

RUSSELL: Oh, yeah. Well, listen to this: I'm not going to study for this test!

TED: So what else is new?

RUSSELL: Oh, but you misunderstand me, young Thompson. This is not passive neglect, but active defiance.

TED: Huh? What are you talking about?

RUSSELL: I'm talking about a protest.

SHEILA: A protest of what?

RUSSELL: A protest of an unfair homework assignment given on the night of Centerville's biggest game of the year.

TED: I had no idea you were such a fan, Russell.

RUSSELL: Oh, sure. I just love it when our guys have the basketball and they make a fast break down the infield for a touchdown.

TED: Very funny.

SHEILA *(slowly and thoughtfully)*: Do you really think that if we all flunked tomorrow, old Whitaker would give us another chance? That would mean I could go to the game, AND pass history.

RUSSELL: You heard what he said: if we look bad, he looks bad.

TED: B-b-but, somebody's sure to tell him what's going on. We'll all get caught.

SHEILA: Not if we all keep our mouths shut, Ted. Do you want to miss the game?

RUSSELL: C'mon, Thompson. Where's your team spirit? Rah, rah, for old Centerville High!

SHEILA: Yeah. Rah, rah, rah!

RUSSELL: Let's vote. All in favor of flunking the test tomorrow so we don't have to study tonight, raise your hands.

(Russell puts up his hand, then Sheila raises hers. They scan the room. One by one, other kids raise their hands, each looking around to make sure everyone else is raising their hands, too. Finally, only Thompson doesn't have his hand up. But slowly he knuckles under and lifts his hand.)

RUSSELL: Well. Looks like it's unanimous.

SOUND EFFECT: School bell.

RUSSELL: See you tomorrow, gang.

(All exit.)

Scene Two

———————————■———————————

Same room, the next day. The students are just finishing their tests. Sheila gets up and takes her paper to the teacher's desk. Mr. Whitaker, who is grading papers, looks somewhat agitated.

SHEILA: Here's my test, Mr. Whitaker.

MR. WHITAKER: Thanks, Sheila. *(Sheila turns to go back to her seat.)* Say, wait a second. You answered all these questions true or false.

SHEILA: What's wrong with that?

MR. WHITAKER: This wasn't a true-and-false test. It was multiple choice.

SHEILA: Oh. . . . Well, you pass a few, you flunk a few!

MR. WHITAKER *(by this time all the papers are in except Ted's)*: The fact is, a few more of you than usual flunked this test—for the second time. I've been looking over every one of the papers as you've given them to me, and everyone's failed but Ted.

RUSSELL *(spinning in his seat to look at Ted, as everyone else glares at Ted also)*: Ted passed?!

TED *(looking quickly up from his paper)*: Only because I haven't finished yet. *(Gets up and takes paper to Mr. Whitaker.)* Here you go, Mr. Whitaker. I'm sure you'll find this one just as unsatisfactory as the others.

MR. WHITAKER: I'm sure I will. Will someone please tell me what's going on here? *(pause)* Didn't anybody study for this test? *(pause)* Sheila?

SHEILA *(hanging her head)*: Er, no, sir.

MR. WHITAKER: Well, why not?

SHEILA: Because I went to the game, like everybody else. I thought it was very unfair of you to expect us to study for such an important test on the night of the big game.

MR. WHITAKER: Why did you risk flunking this quarter just to go to a game?

SHEILA: Well, everybody was going to be there and I didn't want to miss out.

MR. WHITAKER: I wish you kids would care a little less about the opinions of your peers and a little more about things that are really important—like grades. When the teachers get together in the lounge to talk about how well their students are doing, I'm going to be *really* embarrassed about this one!

RUSSELL: Excuse me, sir, but are you saying that if we all started doing good work it would make the other teachers think more of you? I thought we weren't supposed to be interested in the opinions of our peers.

MR. WHITAKER: Well, I . . .

SHEILA: Mr. Whitaker . . . I admit we did the wrong thing today by flunking this test again. But it *is* unfair to want us to get higher grades just so that *you* will look better.

MR. WHITAKER *(after a pause)*: I'm afraid you have a point there, Sheila.

RUSSELL: You should be ashamed of yourself.

SHEILA: Russell!

TED: That's alright, Mr. Whitaker. *(looking at Russell)* I know what it's like to have everybody breathing down your neck.

MR. WHITAKER: Well, I'm afraid I have to record these test scores. But I think we'll work on this material some more next week and give us *all* another chance.

SHEILA: What are you going to tell the other teachers?

MR. WHITAKER: What do you think?

SHEILA: I think maybe we'd all better stop paying so much attention to what other people think.

MR. WHITAKER: I think that's a good idea.

SOUND EFFECT: School bell.

MR. WHITAKER: See you Monday, kids. Class dismissed.

The Holy Ghost Players *are part of Jesus People USA, a community of Christians ministering in the ghettos of Chicago. Through comedy and drama, the H. G. Players have presented Christ to hundreds of groups across the country over the last 12 years.*

□

Let's Be Friends

Photo by Christipher Postel

A   W E E K E N D   R E T R E A T

Breakaway

Aim

Overview

You'll need

B Y B I L L S T E A R N S

To help kids sense the value of friendships with members of the opposite sex without the overtones of romance.

Friendship is fragile stuff; and genuine friendship between members of the opposite sex is especially fragile since our culture insists that male-female relationships be romantic.

Realize that kids are afraid of investing heavily in nonromantic guy-girl friendships. Having same-sex friends and adding a boyfriend or girlfriend is a familiar pattern; but developing nonromantic guy-girl friendships seems weird.

You're bucking some industrial-strength, cultural mind blocks when you ask the Lord—in one weekend—to convince kids to relate as genuine friends with the opposite sex. This retreat focuses on the values of friendship and teaches the truth about masculinity and femininity. It encourages kids to deny their old selves and to reach out in actions that embody Godly qualities. It shows that true friendship is practical even in our romance/sex-saturated society.

☐ Bibles
☐ songbooks or lyrics written on flip charts
☐ Jawbreakers candy
☐ Friendship Crossword Puzzle (activity piece BR1 from the back of this book)
☐ Do-It-Yourself Discussion Guide (activity piece BR2)
☐ Charades Verses (activity piece BR3)
☐ poster boards and markers
☐ construction paper
☐ pencils, crayons
☐ scissors, glue
☐ old magazines
☐ student notebooks
☐ optional: video equipment

SCHEDULE

Friday

8:00 p.m.	Arrive
8:30 p.m.	Games, crowd breakers
9:00 p.m.	Session I
9:45 p.m.	Snack break
10:00 p.m.	Free time or night hike
11:30 p.m.	In-cabin prayer
Midnight	Lights out

Saturday

7:30 a.m.	Prayer session for early risers
8:00-8:30 a.m.	Breakfast
9:00 a.m.	Session II
10:00-10:15 a.m.	Personal devotions
10:30-11:45 a.m.	Organized games

Noon	Lunch
1:00-4:00 p.m.	Recreation, free time
4:00-4:45 p.m.	Session III
5:00 p.m.	Dinner
6:00-6:45 p.m.	Free time
7:00 p.m.	Session IV
9:00 p.m.	Snack, free time
10:30 p.m.	Sing and share
11:30 p.m.	In-cabin prayer
Midnight	Lights out

Sunday

7:30 a.m.	Prayer session for early risers
8:00 a.m.	Breakfast
9:00-10:00 a.m.	Session V
10:30-11:00 a.m.	Worship
11:15 a.m.	Cleanup, pack
Noon	Lunch and depart

Games, Crowd Breakers

Play games that involve relational, group contact. For example, *blob tag* begins with one person "it." Each one caught joins hands with "it" until the whole blob of participants is "it." Or have several guy-girl groups stand in circles, place hands in the center, grasp a hand of two different people and then try to untangle—without breaking hands—into a circle. Play games such as softball, volleyball, basketball, broom hockey, etc. with participants hanging on to each other in mixed-sex clusters of three or four. Get even shy types used to the idea that guys and girls can interact and touch nonsexually.

Session I

Pass out Jawbreakers; distribute colors to identify team groups of five or six. Include members of both sexes on each team. Try to divide couples, but don't be hard nosed about this. (You won't separate kids until later.)

Sole survivor interview. Pick a kid who is imaginative and a good sport. After a song session, introduce this individual as a person who survived shipwreck on an island paradise, who lived for 80 years without contact with any human. Ask, "What did you do first?" "What next?" and so on. Push the interview to the obvious point that all alone, life got dull and lonely.

Visualization. Instruct the kids to close their eyes and relax. Use your imagination to lead them on a tour of their town after a neutron bombing of the entire planet has destroyed all human and animal life but left buildings intact. Let them feel the fun of doing anything they want; let them feel the eventual sadness of having no one to enjoy activities with. End the somber feeling of the tour by having participants open a creaking door to find . . . the alive retreat group! Have them open their eyes. Ask them what they would do and how they would feel when they found each other. Emphasize that isolation is a dead end.

Scripture search on friendship. Divide kids into teams by the Jawbreaker colors on their tongues. Allow teams to complete the "Friendship Crossword Puzzle" (activity piece BR1 from the back of this book).

Call time and ask teams for answers (Across: 1—king; 3—friendship; 5—sharp; 6—curses; 8—Jesus; 9—always. Down: 1—kindness; 2—brother; 4—Christ's; 7—evil). God says good friendships are possible and important.

The talk of the century. **Would you like a friend who treated you like:**

List the qualities of a loving friend found in I Corinthians 13:4-8a. For each quality, give a one-sentence definition that's Biblically accurate (prepare these beforehand). Next, call on previously selected youth and/or adults to share examples of each quality in action.

Wouldn't it be great to spend 80 years on an island paradise with a group of friends who cared about you with those qualities? Can only people from your ethnic group have those qualities? Only people of your exact age? Only people of your same sex?

This weekend you'll learn how to enjoy real friendships with people of the opposite sex without all the drama of romance, without the thrills and chills of the dating game. Write this one down: Learning to be nonromantic, real friends with the opposite sex, is more important than learning how to date.

Session II

After two songs, form the same teams as last night.

Dramatics. Assign each team at least one of the loving-friend qualities from I Corinthians 13. Give about 15 minutes for each team to plan and rehearse a skit and a commercial. Teams should use all members in both. The skit should demonstrate the assigned quality in a guy-girl, nonromantic friendship. The commercial should use the opposite quality to sell its product. For example, a group with "doesn't brag" might do a skit in which a guy says, "My sports trophies aren't really very important to me; I'm more interested in hearing who you think you'll be in about 30 years." Then the team breaks to a commercial in which a diet of "Super Muscle Munchies" builds up a guy's biceps, so that all the girls ooh and ahh while he flexes. Point out that the media's depictions of guy-girl relationships usually encourage qualities opposite those of true friendship.

If you have the equipment, videotape the skits and commercials to show during Session III and back home. If you don't videotape, have the teams present their skits and commercials.

Posters. Next, each team makes two posters. The girls on the team make one that gives the message that they like guys who display the quality assigned their team (For example, "The guys we want for friends don't show off!"). The guys should make a poster giving the same message about girls. Hang the posters up throughout the retreat area.

Personal Devotions
Encourage each participant to read I Corinthians 13:4-8a seven times and to pray for those qualities.

Session III

(If you videotaped the skits and commercials, show them now.)

Group discussions. Remind the group that our society focuses on self. It tells us that to form relationships we must tantalize people's physical and egotistical desires. We must look as attractive as possible.

God's qualities of loving friendship all seem to say, "Forget yourself."

Pass out copies of the "Do-It-Yourself Discussion Guides" (activity piece BR2) and allow about 20 minutes for the teams to compile the information. Call them together to present their findings. Emphasize the importance of new-self values and actions in establishing quality friendships between guys and girls (or anybody else). Be alert for opportunities to explain to participating non-Christians how God can put that new nature within anyone.

Session IV

Play crowd breakers and sing for about 45 minutes.

Collages. Have each team create two collages using old magazines. The first collage should show how the old self relates to people of the opposite sex. The second collage should show how the new self relates. Have teams explain their collages.

Point out that God wants us to relate to everyone—including the opposite sex—according to the new-self qualities.

Girls, think of how many guys could be true friends if they didn't have to be branded as romantic boyfriends. You'd find out a lot of honest stuff about the way guys are when they're not trying to impress girls. And the same holds true for guys. If you can ignore all the world-system messages about sex and ego, there are a bunch of good friends available to you.

Charades. Review the rules of charades. Then have the group divide into the usual teams. Cut up and distribute a set of the Charades Verses (activity piece BR3) to each team. Each team member is to choose a slip of paper and pantomime the command given on it until his or her team guesses its basic idea.

Challenge. Challenge kids to practice those commands regardless of the other person's sex. Ask kids to exchange compliments, handshakes, and hugs after the concluding prayer.

Session V

Have the youth form their teams. Questions kids have about the opposite sex are answered most honestly by people they're not romantically attached to.

Questions and answers. With each team in a circle, toss any object to a participant. Whoever has the object must ask a question of the opposite sex, and team members of that sex have to give answers to the satisfaction of the questioner. He or she then tosses the object to any other team member who asks a question, and so on. Give some sample questions, such as, "How can a girl be nice to a guy without him getting the idea she's attracted to him?" Warn kids against asking questions that would be embarrassing or objectionable.

Allow about 15 minutes for this activity.

Songwriting. Direct each team to use ideas from the weekend to write a verse to the tune of a familiar song.

The Wrap-up. After 15 minutes, have each team sing its song. Then review each session.

■ **What are the advantages of being nonromantic friends with the opposite sex?**

(It allows you to practice the truth that love isn't a feeling—it's a Biblical pattern of action and attitude.)

■ **How can we express love to friends of the opposite sex without falling into old-self lust and selfishness?**

Suggest that kids affirm their relationships in nonromantic terms, avoid spending lots of time alone, try mob dates (see Campolo article), and practice nonromantic touching (pats on the arms, arm over shoulder, one-squeeze hugs, silly handshakes).

■ **What are some advantages of guy-girl friendships?**

(Good place to learn honesty in relationships.)

■ **Why are guy-girl friendships a good way to learn about the opposite sex?**

(Girls know most about girls and vice versa. Safer than the wildness of romance.)

Worship

Focus your brief worship time on the fact that God—who is neither male nor female—constantly demonstrates His love toward us regardless of our attractiveness, of what we can do, of what we have, and even regardless of our response to Him. We can then love others in unselfish, nonromantic ways, "because he first loved us" (I John 4:19). Allow plenty of time for spontaneous sharing from the group.

Warn that the emotional climate of the retreat will wear off—in a week or so group members won't feel as close as they do now. But the wearing off of feelings is no reason to let commitments to real friendships wear off too. □

□

Bill Stearns, *a free-lance writer in Dallas, Texas, has 15 years' experience in youth ministry.*

Friendship Puzzles

Choose a proverb or several proverbs that help solve each of these puzzles. Be able to explain why the proverbs are helpful.

PUZZLE 1

A friend of yours takes you aside one day and says, "I'm worried about you. You're spending a lot of time with some kids that are just bad news. They're going to get you in trouble, I know. I wish you wouldn't hang around with them." How do you respond to this friend? Is he or she meddling in your affairs, or acting as a real friend?

PUZZLE 2

You have a friend who is not very popular with other kids. It's partly his fault—he dresses like a slob, tells stupid jokes that no one understands, and is sometimes very critical of others. You and he grew up on the same street and have known each other for a long time. He considers you his friend. Every so often you can tell he really does feel hurt when others reject him or make fun of him. He really wants to be accepted, but he doesn't know what to do. What should you do or say?

PUZZLE 3

A girl in your class really gets to you. She seems to have everything—good looks, clothes, a car, lots of money to spend, exciting vacation trips. Of course, she has plenty of friends, too. Everyone wants to spend time with her. What should your attitude be toward her? Toward yourself? Why?

Fantasy Friends

Imagine how you would behave in your role in the following situations, and then act it out with your group members. Try to use the skills of trusting, listening, and being trustworthy.

AT SCHOOL

Roles: Student 1, Student 2 (a girl), Girl's Locker

Student 1 is walking down the school hallway. In the distance, he/she sees a girl standing by a locker. It appears that she is crying. Student 1 does not recognize her. What does he/she do? What happens next?

AT CHURCH

Roles: Chris, Sandy, Older Person

Chris is sitting in church, waiting for the service to begin. An older person is sitting to one side of Chris. Then Sandy comes and sits on the other side. Chris has never spoken to Sandy before; Sandy is shy and quiet, spends a lot of time alone, and doesn't seem to have any friends. Sandy doesn't even look at Chris. What does Chris do? What happens next?

I'VE GOT A PROBLEM

PROBLEM ONE

■

"I'm so mad at my mother. She won't let me go to the concert. Just because I made one mistake last fall and came home late. Now she doesn't trust me. She thinks I'm going to do something bad. No matter where I go, she is always suspicious."

RESPONSES

■

A. I met your mother once. She really seems like a creep!

B. I know how you feel. My dad is the same way. I guess parents are just that way. They can't help worrying about you.

C. You shouldn't talk like that. The Bible says that you are supposed to honor your father and mother. You disobeyed them before, so now you have to pay the consequences.

D. Do you think you could somehow get your mother to trust you again? What could you do to prove you're responsible?

E. Listen. Make a deal with your mother. Tell her you'll clean up the whole yard if she lets you go to the concert.

PROBLEM TWO

■

"I feel confused. All my friends know what they are going to do after they graduate—except me. I thought about joining the Air Force, but I'm not sure I want to sign up for so many years. I just don't know what I want to do. Is there something wrong with me?"

RESPONSES

■

A. Yeah, you'd better grow up. If you don't get your act together, life's going to pass you by.

B. What interested you about the Air Force? Do you think you should investigate it more? Maybe it isn't as bad as you think.

C. I know what you should do. Go to the community college for two years. Take some computer classes. That way you can always get a good job until you decide what you really want to do.

D. Look, these things take time. Don't worry. Something will come along that you will really like.

E. I know what you mean. I feel confused, too, sometimes. It's a big decision. I talked with my dad, and he said he had a hard time choosing a direction, also. He's helping me look at some of my options.

RESPONDING 'YOU' OR 'I'

HERE'S THE SITUATION

■

You usually eat lunch with a certain friend in the cafeteria. But this past week he's been eating with a more popular group at another table, with no room for you.

How can you respond? Here are two possibilities:

Response A: "You don't want me around at lunch anymore, I see, now that you're so popular."
    This response assumes the worst about the other person's actions.

Response B: "I feel kind of hurt and left out when you eat at another table with no room for me."

This response states the facts, and gives the friend room to explain his actions or perhaps apologize. The problem still needs to be worked out. But it can be worked out in a better spirit.

As we've just seen, there are at least two ways to express a problem or hurt to a friend: with an "I" statement or a "you" statement. When you use a "you" response, it often starts with the word "you." You accuse the other person of deliberately doing something wrong or hurtful to you. An "I" response usually starts with the word "I," and just expresses the facts: the other person's actions, and your feelings about those actions. It gives the friend the benefit of the doubt. It doesn't immediately force your friend to defend himself/herself. And it may save a friendship!

OVERCOMING
PROVERBS

A gossip betrays a confidence,

but a trustworthy man keeps a secret.
Proverbs 11:13

He who covers over an offense promotes love,

but whoever repeats the matter separates close friends.
Proverbs 17:9

A man of many companions may come to ruin,

but there is a friend who sticks closer than a brother.
Proverbs 18:24

Do not make friends with a hot-tempered man,

do not associate with one easily angered.
Proverbs 22:24

Kisses of an enemy may be profuse

but faithful are the wounds of a friend.
Proverbs 27:6

Perfume and incense bring joy to the heart,

and the pleasantness of one's friend springs from his earnest counsel.
Proverbs 27:9

Friends in *Love*

"Love is patient, love is kind. It does not envy, it does not boast, it is not proud. It is not rude, it is not self-seeking, it is not easily angered, it keeps no record of wrongs. Love does not delight in evil but rejoices with the truth. It always protects, always trusts, always hopes, always perseveres"
I Corinthians 13:4-7, NIV.

List at least ten qualities of love that you find in this passage of Scripture. Then look back at the list of obstacles to friendship that you brainstormed and write in how these qualities of love can help overcome those obstacles.

Qualities of *Love*

HOW THEY CAN OVERCOME THESE OBSTACLES:

1.

2.

3.

4.

5.

6.

7.

8.

9.

10.

A LITTLE HEAVENLY PRESSURE

One night you are awakened at 2:00 A.M. by a bright light at the foot of your bed. As you rub your eyes and try to convince yourself that this must be a dream, the source of the light, an angel, introduces himself.

ANGEL: Hi. I'm Burt, your angel for today, and I've come with good news.

SENIOR HIGH: An angel? With good news? Are you sure you've got the right house?

ANGEL: Are you implying that an angel of the Lord can make mistakes?

SENIOR HIGH: Well, no. It just seems . . . .

ANGEL: Listen. Just show a little respect to someone who's bringing you a message from God.

SENIOR HIGH: You've talked with God . . . about me?

ANGEL: Well, we don't actually get to talk with God. He just gives us orders, and we get to serve Him and praise Him. But for some reason that I'll never understand, you humans are the ones who get to talk with Him. In fact, I'm here in answer to one of your prayers.

SENIOR HIGH: Really? Which one?

ANGEL: Remember a few weeks ago? You felt real bad about something you'd done, so you told Him that it would be a whole lot easier to live the Christian life if only you had a Christian friend to help you.

SENIOR HIGH: I prayed for that? That's not a bad prayer.

ANGEL: Yeah, He told me that humility wasn't one of your real strengths yet. Anyway, He heard your prayer, and I'm here to be your good Christian friend for a while.

SENIOR HIGH: Really? I'm gonna have an angel for my best friend?

ANGEL: Yeah, only I'm not going to be doing angelic-type things while I'm here. I'm just going to be your friend. You know, we'll hang around together. I'll be with you at school, in the locker room, at parties. Stuff like that.

SENIOR HIGH: Whoa. Wait a minute. You're an angel. Angels can't go to parties. In fact, I don't think you'd even feel real comfortable in our locker room.

ANGEL: Well, I know it won't be Heaven. But we'll be together, so you'll be able to stand strong and do the things you know are right, instead of what the people around you are telling you to do.

SENIOR HIGH: You mean I'm going to have to live my life watched all the time by an angel?

ANGEL: No, I won't be just watching. I'll be helping you. Your friends are the ones who are watching you—to see if you live up to their expectations.

SENIOR HIGH: Good point. But still, I don't know about this. What are my friends going to say if I let you help me live the kind of life you're talking about?

ANGEL: They'll probably say you're different.

SENIOR HIGH: Yeah, you're right about that. (He takes a moment to think.)

ANGEL: Is anything wrong?

SENIOR HIGH: No . . . . It's just that I don't know how my friends are going to take this. Could I think about this arrangement for a little while? Maybe I can do okay on my own.

ANGEL: God never forces His help on anyone. But are you sure about this?

SENIOR HIGH: Yeah. I'm pretty sure I can do it. Besides, the people I hang around with are pretty good guys. They could probably give me help if I need it.

ANGEL: You're going to look to your locker room friends for help?

SENIOR HIGH: Yeah.

ANGEL: Then before I go, let me just say, "Good luck." I think you're going to need it.

Pressure vs. Promises

Sometimes our ability to experience God's promises is limited by whether or not we fulfill the conditions of those promises. For instance, in the first reference below, we will be wise (promise) provided we walk with other wise people (condition). Peer pressure often tells us that God's conditions are stupid and that we're stupid if we follow them. But often, if we follow peer pressure, we lose the reward of God's promise.

For each verse below, write an example of the kind of pressure you might experience that would go against God's condition and cause you to lose God's promise. For the first one you might say, "A bunch of guys might ask me to ride in a car 90 miles an hour, at night, with the lights out." That would be peer pressure, asking you to walk with not very wise men.

VERSE	CONDITION	PRESSURE	PROMISE
1. Prov. 13:20	Walk with wise men		You will be wise
2. Prov. 3:6	Put God first in everything you do		He will crown your efforts with success
3. Jas. 5:16	Admit your faults to other Christians		You will be healed
4. Lk. 6:36	Forgive others		You will be forgiven
5. Mt. 10:32	Acknowledge Jesus before your friends		He will acknowledge you before God
6. Eph. 6:2, 3	Honor your parents		You will have a long and happy life
7. Mal. 3:10	Give your tithes and offerings to God		He will give generously to you
8. Lk. 6:35	Love your enemies		Your reward will be great
9. Jn. 13:35	Love other Christians		God honors us as His disciples
10. Isa. 26:3	Keep your mind on God		He will give you perfect peace

BY STEVE LAWHEAD
STUCK INSIDE

There is an invisible sign in the middle
of the cafeteria.
  It reads:
  Property of the Senior Class Social-
ites—
  All Others Keep Out!
Although the sign is invisible,
  everyone can read it.
  Everyone knows and obeys.
There are other posted territories:
  the far end of the student concourse
  near the drinking fountain,
  the grassy hill in front of
  the school entrance.
No trespassing! Keep Out!
This area belongs to us!
Belonging.
  That's what those invisible signs
mean.
To those on the inside
  they form the boundaries of a
refuge,
  an island of safety
  in a sea of self-consciousness.
From the security of our island
  in the middle of the lunchroom
  I sometimes feel guilty as I look out
  at the loners.
They sit alone, eat alone.
Or they slouch unobtrusively behind
their books
  and act like they're studying.
But they're not studying;
  they're watching us.
Their eyes betray them;
I've seen the looks of unguarded
  envy they throw our way.
They are saying, "If only I could
  join the group . . . ."
But it's impossible;
There are unwritten rules governing
  these things.

I can only imagine what the outsiders
  are feeling.
Yet some days there is a split second
  of uncertainty just before I
  reach my group.
I wonder,
  What if they don't recognize me?
  What if they don't let me in?
But I approach and the ranks open to
  admit me.
  I slap my tray down and I'm in—
  safe inside for another day.

I have learned to play the games
  you have to play to fit in.
I know all the moves, the rules, the
  talk.
I wear the mask the group wears
  and never, never let anyone see the
  real me.
There's security there:
  I'm in, I belong.
  As long as I go along
  with the group—
  do as they do,
  act as they act,
  think as they think.

Those are the rules.
  Break them and you're out.
  Then you'll be a loner
  holding your tray
  and looking for a place to sit.
  On the outside looking in.
I sometimes argue with the guilt:
Is it my fault for enjoying what
  everyone wants?
What am I supposed to do?
Quit?
If I quit the group what good would
  that do?
  Who would that help?
Could I just walk away and be
  myself?
Deep inside I know the answer.
  Deep inside I must admit the truth:
  I need the clique;
  I'm too afraid to stand alone,
  to be myself.
My fear keeps me tied to the group.

Still, I'm haunted by the eyes of
  the outsiders.
  They're always watching.
I used to think they could tell I
  was different,
  that even though I ran with the
  group,
  I still had my own identity.
Now, I'm not so sure.
Last week I saw a kid in the library—
  one of those who sits alone
  at lunch and studies
  while we're all cutting up.
We were looking for the same book,
  he and I.
We saw it at the same instant and
  reached for it.

I got there first.
I looked at his eyes
  behind the thick glasses
  and felt a little sorry for him.
I wanted to do a friendly thing
  so I offered the book to him.
He looked at it, then at me, and turned
  his back.
As he walked away I heard him
  mumbling to himself.
The others said the kid was a stuck-up
  snob when I told them.
Funny, that's what he'd muttered
  about me.

Why do we have to have these
  cliques?
Why can't we all just be ourselves?
unself-conscious.
  Not pretending to be the laughing,
  careless and cool people we're not.
What is everyone afraid of?
I wonder.
If I decided to take one lunch hour
  and sit with a loner,
  what would happen?
  What if we all did that?
There'd be a revolution—a quiet
  revolution.
  And a lot of people
  would be freed that day.
But I don't look for anything like
  that to happen.
  It's just too hard.
I don't want to be rejected,
  but neither do I want to be part of
  a circle of turned backs
  that says, "You're not one of us."
A choice must be made.
  I can see that now.
It would be better
  if one or two of my friends
  in the group saw that, too.
Maybe they do.
Maybe they feel
  the same way I feel:
  trapped,
  stuck in the clique,
  but not daring to leave.
Maybe they're waiting
  for someone to break free,
  to step out and risk something new.
There's one good way to find out.

FRIENDSHIP

CROSSWORD PUZZLE

As a team, look up each reference; then fill in the blanks. Remember that the exact word needed might not appear in your translation of the Bible, so use your imagination!

ACROSS

1. Proverbs 22:11. If you've got nothing to hide, even authorities like this can be friends.

3. Psalm 41:9. _____ is risky since a friend can turn against you; but the risk is worth it!

5. Proverbs 27:17. A good friend can make you _____.

6. Proverbs 27:14. If you're insensitive to a friend's needs (such as sleeping late), he or she might think your blessings are really _____.

8. Matthew 11:19. Who's the classic example of befriending even unattractive people?

9. Proverbs 17:17. A friend loves you when?

DOWN

1. Job 6:14. Something a friend owes a friend.

2. Proverbs 18:24. As a friend, God sticks closer than a _____.

4. John 15:13-15. Whose friend are you?

7. I Corinthians 15:33. We can be messed up by this kind of friend.

IF YOU FINISH EARLY, brainstorm and list the top twenty qualities of a real friend.

DO-IT-YOURSELF
DISCUSSION GUIDE

Have your group assign someone to read each question. (How about somebody who doesn't know how to count to three in French?) Have this person read a question and then discuss it briefly. Don't feel pressured to figure out everything about each topic. Jot down any complex questions you have to blast your youth workers with later!

 ONE Forgetting yourself and reaching out to others are keys to building relationships. But how can you forget yourself? Take a vote on who agrees or disagrees and discuss the statement: "It's impossible to forget about yourself."

 TWO Look up and discuss what the following passages tell you about yourself. Remember that different translations sometimes use different English words to describe the same thing. Luke 9:23; Luke 14:26; Romans 6:6; Ephesians 4:22; Colossians 3:9.

 **THREE** As a Christian, you have a new self that's controlled by God's Spirit. Your new self has what it takes to build real friendships that have no barriers to people of another race, age, or sex. Read and discuss: Ephesians 4:23, 24; Colossians 3:10; Galatians 5:22-26.

 **FOUR** How do you forget or "deny" or "lay aside" your old self and step into your new Spirit-controlled self? Read and discuss I John 1:9. Notice how the surrounding verses mention walking in darkness (old self) and light (new self).

 FIVE Join hands and silently pray as a group that God will help you understand these basic ideas.

If you realize you're stuck in your old self because you're not a Christian, be sure to talk to one of the adults on the retreat tonight.

Charades VERSES

Explain that this is something a good friend does for his or her friends.

Act out: **MAKE THEM FEEL IMPORTANT.**

After your team has guessed this commandment (or after you've given up trying to make the lamebrains get it!) read to them Philippians 2:3, 4.

Explain that this is something a good friend does for his or her friends.

Act out: **CARRY THEIR BURDENS.**

After your team has guessed this commandment (or after you've given up trying to make the lamebrains get it!) read to them Galatians 6:2.

Explain that this is something a good friend does for his or her friends.

Act out: **DO GOOD.**

After your team has guessed this commandment (or after you've given up trying to make the lamebrains get it!) read to them Galatians 6:10.

Explain that this is something a good friend does for his or her friends.

Act out: **TELL THE TRUTH WITH LOVE.**

After your team has guessed this commandment (or after you've given up trying to make the lamebrains get it!) read to them Ephesians 4:15.

Explain that this is something a good friend does for his or her friends.

Act out: **BE KIND.**

After your team has guessed this commandment (or after you've given up trying to make the lamebrains get it!) read to them Ephesians 4:32.

Explain that this is something a good friend does for his or her friends.

Act out: **FORGIVE.**

After your team has guessed this commandment (or after you've given up trying to make the lamebrains get it!) read to them Ephesians 4:32.

Explain that this is something a good friend does for his or her friends.

Act out: **GIVE TO THEIR NEEDS.**

After your team has guessed this commandment (or after you've given up trying to make the lamebrains get it!) read to them Romans 12:13.

Explain that this is something a good friend does for his or her friends.

Act out: **BE HAPPY WITH THEM.**

After your team has guessed this commandment (or after you've given up trying to make the lamebrains get it!) read to them Romans 12:15.

Explain that this is something a good friend does for his or her friends.

Act out: **CRY WITH THEM.**

After your team has guessed this commandment (or after you've given up trying to make the lamebrains get it!) read to them Romans 12:15.